# ROMAN WALES

## SARAH SYMONS

# Acknowledgements

I wish to express my grateful thanks to Mrs Kay Kays of the National Museum & Galleries of Wales, Cardiff; Dr Mark Lewis of the Legionary Museum, Caerleon; Mr Oliver Blackmore, Curator of the Newport Museum & Art Gallery; Mr Gavin Evans of the County Museum, Abergwili, Carmarthen; Ms Laura Pooley of the Grosvenor Museum, Chester; and Mrs Susan Hill of the Glamorgan-Gwent Archaeological Trust for providing images or giving permission to print those taken at the museums, and similarly to Mr Alun Pritchard of the National Trust, Bangor for permission to use the images of the Dolocothi Gold Mines, and also to Cadw for their kind permission to use images.

I would also like to thank the attentive staff of the photographic department of Boots Limited, Swansea.

First published 2015

Amberley Publishing
The Hill, Stroud
Gloucestershire, GL5 4EP

www.amberley-books.com

British Library Cataloguing in Publication Data.
A catalogue record for this book is available from the British Library.

ISBN 978 1 4456 4380 9 (paperback)
ISBN 978 1 4456 4407 3 (ebook)

Typeset in 10pt on 13pt Sabon.
Typesetting and Origination by Amberley Publishing.
Printed in the UK.

# Contents

# Introduction

When the Roman army invaded Wales in AD 74, they had to build a continuous chain of fortresses throughout the length and breadth of the country to suppress the fierce opposition they were receiving from the tribal population. After conquering the country in AD 79, the fortresses effectively played an important role in establishing civilian settlements, which grew into some of the prosperous towns we know today such as Caerleon, Carmarthen and Chester. But because of the constant building throughout the centuries, other towns such as Usk, Abergavenny and Neath have not survived, having been buried beneath the new buildings of post-Roman Wales. Luckily, through modern technology, we have been given an insight into the past of those towns whose foundations could be successfully excavated. They have provided us with a wealth of information as to how the conquered Celts embraced the Roman way of life, and, by looking at the personal and domestic items they left behind, we have been able to glance back into their lives and even learn how they decorated their homes.

The conquest of Wales was extremely important to the Romans. It was a country rich in agricultural land, which was essential for providing food for the Roman army. The knowledge that Wales was also rich in minerals such as copper and gold was another incentive to conquer and settle, especially when gold was to be had. The Romans exploited this to the full by filling their dwindling treasury coffers, providing themselves with currency to pay for luxuries and their expanding armies. Invading other countries and keeping their army well fed and equipped was a costly business.

After the conquest of Wales, Julius Agricola, the first Roman Governor of Britain, decreed that the Celts should embrace the Roman way of life with its emphasis on law and order. As a result the conquered tribes soon discovered that there were benefits to be gained from the conquest, even though they were captive in their own country. To defy the Romans would have been counterproductive and would have led to more bloodshed.

One of the benefits to the Romanised housewife was the introduction of new products such as wine and olive oil for cooking and lighting, and different vegetables such as onions, turnips, cabbage and leeks. Figs, dates and other exotic fruit arriving from the Mediterranean also offered a more varied diet. She possessed better earthenware and ate from high-class pottery imported from the Continent by the Romans. However, from the large quantities of quernstones found, she continued with the tradition of grinding her own corn to make flour. More importantly, under the Romans, the Celts soon learned to read and write. Latin inscriptions made by the soldiers were the only writing they had seen, but as time passed they were able to understand what these meant. From the number of seal boxes they left behind, we can see that they had also begun to communicate with one another through the written word. The more learned among them prospered to become respected citizens such as councillors and magistrates.

The everyday living standards of the Celts soon changed for the better as their homes evolved from crude structures of thatch and mud into stone-built ones with tiled roofs, tessellated floors and glass windows – never before seen in Britain. Those who prospered were rich enough to decorate their homes with mosaic floors and porticoes and even had underfloor heating – also never before seen in Britain, and not to be seen again until the twentieth century. Even the architectural landscape was changing as the Romans introduced the classical architecture of the colonnaded buildings that graced Rome itself.

Over time, Romanised Wales flourished to become a wealthy province within the Roman Empire, with the production of gold being the main contributing factor – it fed the Roman coffers and helped to finance the growth of the ever-expanding towns.

Few people could write in those early days, as was the case in medieval times when only educated monks were able to chronicle events, so we have learned about the Roman conquest through the writings of the Roman historian Tacitus. As not many structures have survived from the Roman era, we have had to depend on modern archaeology to find out how they once looked. The recent excavations have certainly given us a glimpse back into that historic period and have provided a fascinating picture as to how the people lived, worked and played.

The Romano-British citizen certainly left behind a treasure trove of pottery, glassware and metal implements and, occasionally, mosaic floors and samples of coloured plastered walls have survived, all of which have been beautifully preserved in museums despite having been buried for sixteen centuries. It is therefore to the archaeologists' credit that many of these treasures have been restored to their former beauty to be admired and enjoyed for all time. They are our mirrors into an era that was the foundation of civilisation itself. What was once lost has now been restored to give a good account of its role in Roman times.

1. Map of Roman Wales.

# *Isca Silurum*: Caerleon

Modern Caerleon is a picturesque little village surrounded by an amphitheatre of green hills and lying about five miles from Newport. This was where the Second Augustan Legion of the Roman army chose to build their fortress on the banks of the River Usk. They named it *Isca Silurum* after the river and the Silurian territory in which it was situated. The legion was one of four that had invaded Britain in AD 43, and had come up from Devon, where it had previously been based.

The Silurian territory, in the southern part of Celtic Wales, had been under Roman control ever since they crossed its borders in AD 47. On arrival, the Romans were met with severe opposition from the Silures. The conflict raged on for thirty years. Tacitus, the Roman historian, described the tribe warriors as fierce and valiant, which they were; they became excellent guerrilla fighters and terrorised the invaders whenever they could. In AD 52, the Romans suffered their greatest defeat in Britain when they lost a large part of a legion at the hands of the Silures.

However, as a conquered tribe, the Silures in this area soon settled down to captive life. After all, they had no choice with an army of 6,000 men on their doorstep, and to many it was in their best interests to trade with the soldiers – it brought them some kind

2. Village centre.

of livelihood. The military showed no objection to this arrangement, and neither did they mind some of the people setting up homes outside the walls of the fortress. Over time these homesteads grew into little communities, and they soon merged into one common entity, from which *Civitas Isca* came into being. It became an important centre in this part of Silurian territory, and because it was surrounded by prime agricultural land, its citizens were able to prosper as the town grew. Being sited on the broad Usk with access to the sea and the port of Newport, ships were able to dock right on its doorstep to trade with its neighbours across the Bristol Channel. The River Usk was also a means by which the garrison could receive its essential supplies.

While the Roman fortresses at Usk (*Burrium*), Abergavenny (*Gobannium*) and Neath (*Nidum*) have been located by excavation, their civilian settlements could not be owing to the density of the modern buildings built over them. Nevertheless, a plethora of pottery and personal items were found at each area to give a comprehensive picture of the role of these settlements in the development of Wales under Roman occupation.

However, the early twentieth century excavations of *Isca Silurum* were more successful in that they were able to reveal a greater portion of the legionary fortress and the civilian suburbs that had originated outside its defences. As the fortress was of such momentous importance, it is worth a mention.

## The Legionary Fortress

The legionary fortress at *Isca Silurum* was a major construction, and completely dominated the landscape. Never before had the native Silures seen buildings of such immense proportions. At first these would have intimidated them. The legionary fortress was one of only three built in Roman Britain. The other two were at Chester and York. The fortress was regarded as the most important of the military sites in Europe. It was mentioned in the *Antonine Itinerary*, a second-century Roman travel guide, as *Isca Legio Augusta* (Isca of the Augustan Legion). The legion comprised ten cohorts, each with six centuries of eighty men and commanded by a centurion. The 4,800 men altogether were all elite troops with Roman citizenship. The auxiliary fortresses, on the other hand, had garrisons of only 500 to 1,000 soldiers who had been drawn from the occupied territories. The garrison at Brecon, for instance, consisted of 500 Spanish cavalry. Horse-mounted troops were essential in patrolling the inaccessible mountain terrain and for swift communication between the fortresses. It was estimated that at Caerleon there were around 6,000 troops, which included a force of auxiliary soldiers.

The fortress here covered a mammoth fifty acres, and was enclosed entirely by a defensive wall twenty feet high with turrets and watch towers. It had four entrances, situated at each of the four points of the compass. Like all fortresses, it was built to the same military plan and had a 'playing card' shape with rounded corners. All its internal buildings had also been laid out to a set plan. This enabled troops to be familiar with their location inside the fort whenever they moved from one fort to another. The ramparts were behind the *intervallum*, a strip of narrow land which surrounded the inside of the perimeter, and this gave instant access to ramparts when the need arose.

The legionaries were expert carpenters and stone masons, so the internal buildings were built to a high standard. One of particular note was the *Principia* – the headquarters building which housed the administration offices and was where the legion's standards and ceremonial items were stored. It had a special room called the *sacellum* – the treasury, where all the money was kept. A bust of the emperor would also have been exhibited there. In keeping with the building's importance, the internal walls had been highly decorated with coloured plaster and specially laid floors. Being such an important building on the main street, it had been built to the highest standards, and would have had a colonnaded frontage. A colourful mosaic floor that may have come from the *sacellum* was found in the churchyard under which the headquarters building was located, and is now on display at the Legionary Museum in the centre of Caerleon. Included in its colourful design was a *cantharus*, a Greek vessel for mixing wine.

Next door were the luxurious quarters of the legate, or commander of the legion, built in the style of a Mediterranean villa. This had a central courtyard with its own well, and the legate would also have had his own bathing suite. This would have had special treatment to meet the commander's demands, as befitted his rank.

In order to feed a garrison of this size the fortress would have had several granaries for storing grain. These were extensive timber buildings with raised floors to provide ventilation and keep out the rodents. At Usk, which garrisoned the Twentieth Legion for about three

3. A mosaic found in the headquarters building of the fortress (now at the Legionary Museum).

years before they moved out due to flooding, there had been five large granaries and some smaller ones. It was estimated that the large granaries there had been capable of storing rations for 2,826 men, and the smaller ones enough for 1,625 men. So it is more than likely that with a larger force at Caerleon, its granaries would have been even larger.

Large quantities of charcoal were found in several of the cookhouses. Among this charcoal a small hoard of *denarii* coins was found, comprising eight of Hadrian's reign, three of Faustina, and one of Antoninius Pius, indicating that the cookhouses had functioned until the middle of the second century. A *denarius* was just over a day's pay for a second-century legionary soldier, so someone had been careless with their pay. Fragments of jars, cooking pots and pie dishes also surfaced. Charcoal deposits and iron slag found in a large building with a courtyard suggest that it had been a legionary workshop, with the arrangement of rooms around the courtyard serving as accommodation for the workforce. The fortress was self-sufficient; the soldiers were capable of undertaking their own repairs and maintenance. There would have been an abundance of timber in the nearby woods for carpentry, fuel and making the charcoal on which they cooked.

Circular ovens were found next to the *intervallum*, where the soldiers had prepared their own meals. They were situated there to protect them from the winds and were a safe distance away from the rest of the buildings. An interesting discovery was a stone on which the centurion of the eighth cohort, Valerius Maximus, had inscribed his name. Another such stone to have survived was an altar dedicated to 'Salus Regina' by 'P. Sallienius Thalmus', a prefect of the legion.

Also accommodated within the fortress walls were the barracks, and, as they lay under pasture with no later buildings hindering excavations, their complete internal layout was uncovered and is open to the public.


## The Legionary Barracks

The fully excavated barracks are another of Caerleon's popular open-air attractions, and are situated on the opposite side of the amphitheatre in an area known as Prysg Field. Access to the site is by way of a short walk through the adjoining field running alongside the road.

The barracks were built in the north-west corner of the fortress and were constructed in blocks 250 feet long and thirty-five to forty feet wide. They were grouped in blocks of two, with each pair facing inwards on to a common street that was twenty feet wide. Each block also had twelve double cubicles arranged in strict pairs, side by side for the recruits, and a separate room for the centurion at the end.

Each cubicle in a block accommodated eight men, who slept on bunk beds placed around the walls with a single table for eating in the centre. Each block also had a long veranda, placed on the inner side of the building to protect it from stormy weather. Quantities of window glass were found, which showed that the soldier had been given substantial protection from the inclement weather. As he was responsible for his own armoury and would have to pay for a replacement if it got lost or damaged, he kept it safe in the room next door to his sleeping quarters.

Excavation of the barracks revealed masses of stratified pottery and coins, which showed that they were built during the first century and were occupied well into the third. There was also an abundance of triangular tile antefixes of various kinds that had been nailed on to the eaves for some kind of decoration. The most common image was that of the sun with an eight-spiked wheel above.

An extraordinary discovery was a hoard of five gold *aurei* hidden under the floor of one cubicle. This coin was the highest denomination in the Roman currency and was not circulated widely owing to its high value. It had obviously been saved by one soldier and then hidden for safety. The hoard was regarded as a significant find. The other interesting discovery, found in a centurion's quarters, was a bronze plaque of the winged figure of Victory with a standard in one hand. It was believed to have come off a ceremonial piece of armour. The soldier had possibly kept it as a private shrine. Another keepsake was the statuette of a *genius paterfamilias*, which had been used as a personal good luck charm. Traditionally, the *genius*, or father figure, was venerated as a personal guardian that brought protection to the whole household, and was a kind of a Roman St Christopher. This particular *genius* was shown wearing a flowing toga with its head covered in the drapery and holding a scroll in one hand. At least half of these figures found in Britain can be dated to the third century or later, but only two others have been recovered from military sites; one from Shields and the other from Richborough, Kent, making this yet another significant find.

4. The barracks.

5. Hoard of five *aurei* found in the barracks.

6. A bronze plaque of a Winged Victory found in the barracks at Caerleon.

7. Figure of a *genius paterfamilias* found in the barracks.

Apart from vast quantities of coins, which confirmed that the barracks were still being occupied well into the third century, there were many varieties of pottery including cooking pots and *ollae* – square-shaped dishes for stews. Supposedly, the barracks became vacant during the demise of the fortress around AD 250, when the need for a military presence had diminished and the legion was transferred elsewhere.

To the west of the Prysg Field Barracks was the parade ground where detachments of the legion paraded and practised their fighting techniques.

The soldiers played popular board games of the time and left behind many varieties of dice and gaming counters, mainly cut from bone. Some samples were found at Brecon.

Bathing was a ritual that the Roman citizen took seriously, and this rite was given to the soldiers within the fortress walls, where they also relaxed during their time off duty. The most significant building within the fortress walls was undoubtedly the legionary baths.

## The Legionary Baths

This grand building demonstrated the lengths to which the military went to ensure the wellbeing of its troops, and was the most significant building to be discovered within the fortress walls. Unfortunately, due to the close proximity of the surrounding modern buildings, only one-sixth of this bathing complex could be excavated. Nevertheless, the excavations exposed a wealth of fascinating features which the modern visitor can enjoy from the observation platforms within the covered exhibition hall.

The baths were excavated between 1964 and 1983, during which time it was confirmed from the artefacts found that they had been constructed around AD 75, soon after the legion had settled there, and had been built on a grand scale with vaulted ceilings and several bathing suites. The floor plan also included a large exercise hall, an aisle, and a large courtyard, which had given it an impressive entrance. Within the courtyard was a long, narrow swimming pool (*natatorium*), which had an overall length of 135 feet. This gave it a larger area than the famous one at Bath. It had the capacity to hold 80,230 gallons of water, which was fed through lead piping and was renewed every day after being discharged into the Usk. The swimming pool was later shortened to eighty-six feet, probably after part of the legion was transferred to Hadrian's Wall in AD 130. The brick wall which was used to shorten the pool can still be seen.

An ornate fountain house had once stood at the shallow end of the swimming pool, where water had cascaded down a flight of marble steps. From fragments found during the excavations, the interior of the fountain house had been lavishly decorated, as had the apse, but sadly neither of them had survived. Only the dolphin head through which the water had been ejected survived.

The bathing suites themselves contained the *caldarium* (the hot-water pool), the *tepidarium* (warm pool), and the *frigidarium* (the cold plunge pool), into which the bathers would enter in sequence to complete their bathing process, similar to the Turkish baths of today. The bathers entered through the heated *apodyterium* (changing room), where they stored their clothes. Each suite had alcoves in which were wash basins, where the bathers would splash themselves before covering their bodies with oil and scraping off the dirt with long-handled scrapers called *strigiles*. These were curved to fit the contours of the body and were usually made out of bone, while the scraper itself had been made out of shell and cut to shape. Once the dirt had been scraped off, the bather would then enter the *caldarium* to wash themselves. However, one wealthy bather, probably a senior officer at the fortress, possessed a *strigil* which had been custom made by having the handle inlaid with gold and silver. He had the misfortune of losing it one day, and it would only be found sixteen centuries later. Another bather lost his engraved pot-bellied bottle that had contained his oil. This was found at the same time as the *strigil*.

All the floors within the bathing complex had underfloor heating, which was provided by the hypocaust. This was a method where a furnace was built outside with channels leading into the spaces under the floors held up by brick or stone piers to allow the heat to circulate from the furnace. The *tepidarium* and the *caldarium* were also heated by this method, and it is possible to study this amazing system at close hand inside the exhibition hall.

It is also possible to observe the intricate drainage system the Roman engineers had installed to drain the dirty water into the river. Another special exhibit is the mosaic floor that had once graced one of the bathing suites. This can be seen hanging close to where it was found by the excavators.

The baths underwent drastic changes when by the end of the second century modifications had to be made to combat flooding. All floors throughout the complex were raised. It was at this time that the swimming pool was also shortened.

There then followed a period of neglect, although the baths appeared to have remained operational until the year AD 240. They then fell into disrepair, and long after the Romans had left, the native inhabitants took from the abandoned building whatever stone they required to build their own homes, and even used the baths as a cattle market. It was at this time that Roman *Isca* came into its own, with the citizens progressing with their new lives and claiming much of what the military had left behind to further their own causes. The baths survived as a ruined shell until as late as the eighteenth century, when an Italian artist portrayed them in an engraving which showed that, despite crumbling from decay, their vaulted halls still dominated the skyline and provided a dramatic picture of their one-time splendour.

## *Isca* (Romano-Celtic settlement)

When the legion was withdrawn from the fortress around AD 250, large parts of it were left unoccupied. This gave the native population an opportunity to occupy what buildings they could within the fortress. Its final demise came when the main buildings were demolished around AD 287 and AD 296.

However, not all the soldiers left. Many of the legionaries decided to stay at *Isca* to make a life for themselves by marrying local women and raising families, while others chose to retire in the picturesque surroundings of the suburb of Bulmore to the east of the fortress. Tombstones of those who had died there after years of retirement were found, including one which commemorated the death of Jules Valens, who had died at the ripe old age of 100.

During the third and fourth centuries, the emerging population made use of whatever stone they wanted from the abandoned fortress to build their homes, and they even turned the baths into a cattle market. Thereafter, *Isca* continued to decay, and in the fifth century, medieval Caerleon emerged.

During the excavations at the latter end of the twentieth century, the first signs of *Isca* as a Romano-British settlement came when a complete small neighbourhood consisting of twenty-two dwellings surfaced. All had been constructed with coarse rubble masonry and fronted the main road running north to south. Although they had been roofed with terracotta tiles, their floors were very basic, having been laid with pounded clay to provide a firm surface. Their internal layouts were all different and determined their function as either domestic or industrial. Judging from the deposits of slag found on many floors, some metalworking had taken place. The discovery of other tools suggested that carpentry had also taken place there. It would appear from the remains of horse-and-cart harnesses, a reaping hook and a scythe that agriculture had sustained this little community. Over the years, the floors improved with the addition of laying river pebbles on top of the clay, which, as the owners found, gave them greater firmness. In contrast, the other dwellings that came to light were more architecturally advanced as the inhabitants progressed up the social ladder. On one such dwelling several column bases were found, which suggests that it had possessed a courtyard surrounded by columns. A pleasing discovery was a quantity of coloured wall plaster with many of its colours still preserved brightly. Bricks that had supported the hypocaust had been stamped LEG II AVG, indicating that they had been made at the fortress kilns. The kilns also produced roofing tiles. One such tile, now on display at the Legionary Museum, shows an imprint of the nails from a soldier's sandal as the result of him stepping on the clay while it was wet. Others show imprints of paws from when dogs had been allowed to roam freely around the kilns. The settlements to the south-west of the fortress behind the amphitheatre and parade ground appeared to have been relatively high in status, with shops.

Domestic items such as the high-quality Samian ware suggested that the owners had also dined well. This high-class domestic ware was imported in vast quantities from southern Gaul (France), and had even been the chosen tableware of the high-ranking soldiers at the fortress. It was coloured red and was often decorated with animals and mythological characters. It was also different from other pottery in that it had a glaze. One of the Samian bowls found here had been engraved with gladiatorial scenes surrounded by wild animals. An ornamental buckle with inlaid enamelling was also found and, interestingly, a bunch of keys. All these items are now on display at the Legionary Museum. A water tank was another interesting find at the villa, and indicated that the owners had had their own bathing suite. There were channels running across the walls which had conveyed heat to the rooms, and no doubt heated the bath water.

Another neighbouring residence also had the features of a Roman villa, with rooms surrounding a central courtyard lined with graceful columns. These villas would have been two stories high. Previously, the Celts would not have known having another set of rooms above the ground ones, so when they first began to acquire two-storey residences it must have been quite a novelty. One large building with a courtyard surrounded by rooms and an extension on either side was thought to have been a *mansio*, a guest house for visiting travellers.

8. A roofing tile with imprints of boots at the Caerleon Legionary Museum.

The remains of the hospital also emerged from the excavations. The floors there had been concreted, but the passages had been flagged with ordinary slabs of stone. The rooms had possessed coloured wall plaster, and from the fragments found, it was obvious that special attention had been given to them. The decoration showed the Roman taste in interior decoration at that time, red being a favourite colour. Traces of red lines and a pattern of yellow flowers on a red background were found in some rooms, while others had floral patterns in green, yellow and black. There were also designs made up of red panels edged with green and yellow lines on a white background. Red roofing tiles littered the floors, many of which bore the legion's insignia, LEG II AVG. The legionary kilns also produced domestic pottery for the home, called 'Caerleon ware', and much of it was found around the town, proving its popularity among households. As pottery was manufactured in large quantities, it was not expensive to replace if broken. The Roman *mortarium* was also popular. This was a bowl with a gritty interior for pulverising or grinding food. Over 2,000 shards of this type of vessel were found.

A chance find in the town of an inscription that had recorded the repair of the Temple of Diana in AD 250 by the legion's commanding officer, Postumius Varus, indicated that *Isca* had been well endowed with the classical architecture we have come to associate with Rome. A head of Mithras was also discovered, which suggested the existence of a *Mithraeum*, a temple where the god was worshipped. In reality, Mithras was of Persian origin but was introduced and accepted into the Roman culture in AD 68, and was worshipped throughout the first three centuries. He was the god of light and represented

9. An adornment from a piece of furniture, probably a chair or settee. It is now in the Newport Museum & Art Gallery.

10. Storage jar and amphorae on display at the Legionary Museum.

the power of goodness, promising his followers that they would be recompensed after death for the evil they had suffered in life. In mythology, Mithras was said to have killed the sacred bull from which all life sprung. One of the essential features of a *Mithraeum* was a windowless sunken room to represent the cave in which Mithras had killed the bull. These rooms were lit by burning torches attached to the walls and lined with stone benches on which the congregation sat, probably covered over with furs to make them more comfortable. Unfortunately neither the Temple of Diana nor the *Mithraeum* could be found. Only six Mithraic temples have been discovered in Roman Britain so far. The one at Caerleon would have been a coup for the archaeologists working there.

## The Civic Baths

By adopting to the Roman way of life, *Isca*'s citizens soon benefited from the array of luxuries to which the Romans had introduced them. They soon embraced the Roman culture and possibly even the way of dress by wearing the toga, although it was not entirely suitable for the inclement British weather.

The Romans, who were noted for being pleasure seekers, built two public baths in the style of the fortress ones and provided the new citizens with an outlet for socialising. One set of baths was built outside the southern defences of the fortress and the other outside the south-western defences next to the amphitheatre. However, only a small fraction of the latter baths could be found. The southern baths left many interesting clues as to their function in the new Romano-British society, and as the baths also possessed all the luxurious features of the fortress ones, the new converts soon found the idea of public bathing a pleasurable experience, especially when it included body massage and gambling in the bargain. From the amount of discs and gaming counters found there, this additional attraction had been very popular. Probably a room had been set aside for this pursuit.

The converted Silurian also adopted the Roman deities. One couple had even erected a kind of shrine in the baths asking Fortuna, the patroness of good fortune, to bring good luck (*bono eventus*) to the bathers. It shows the couple standing beneath an archway, and the Latin inscription outlined in red beneath the figures identified them as Cornelius Castus and his wife, Julia Belismicus. The stone is now on display at the Legionary

11. Shrine to Fortuna in the civic baths. Now in the Legionary Museum.

12. Enamel buckles lost in the civic baths. Now in the Legionary Museum.

Museum. Fortuna often figured in bathhouse dedications, since it was thought that nakedness was vulnerable to evil forces and needed protection. A statue of Medusa had also been erected there. She was a Greek mythological character who was transformed into a Gorgon and from whose blood the wings of Pegasus sprung. True to Roman standards, there would also have been marble statuettes standing in little alcoves set around the walls, which would have given the baths a distinctive classical look.

Among the personal items left behind by the bathers and found trapped in the drains were eighty-eight engraved gemstones, which had become loose from ring settings after being submerged in the hot water of the *caldarium*. Enamelled buckles lost by men are also on show at the Legionary Museum.

## The Amphitheatre

This is another of Caerleon's 'masterpieces' from the Roman era which continues to attract visitors every day, and is regarded as being the only significant Roman structure south of Hadrian's Wall. It was yet another feature that delighted the citizens of *Isca* after the Roman soldiers had left, and remained one of the town's most important structures from the time it was built during the reign of Vespasian in AD 77–79 to its apparent

13. Entrance into the amphitheatre.

destruction at the end of the third century. It was situated only fifty feet from the south-west walls of the fortress, where a thriving community had begun to establish itself. It was constructed after the civic baths, as the hypocaust of the baths was in its way and had to be demolished to make way for one of the amphitheatre's entrances.

Oval in shape, it measures 267 by 222 feet overall, and has the distinction of being the only fully excavated amphitheatre in Europe. It was first excavated in 1927–29 by Mortimer Wheeler, the eminent archaeologist of his day, who was later knighted for his services to archaeology.

The amphitheatre was first seen as a depression in the ground surrounded by grassy mounds enclosed within stone walls, and no one knew what they were. In ignorance of the structure's true identity, local people called it 'King Arthur's Round Table', a belief that was handed down through the generations until it became part of local folklore. It was only when archaeology was blossoming as a science that it was decided to investigate what the mounds were, and it was soon discovered that they were banks where spectators had once sat, and that it was indeed an amphitheatre. It was thrilling discovery. A coin of Vespasian found embedded in the mortar soon confirmed the date of its erection as AD 75, at about the same time that the Coliseum was being built in Rome.

In its original form, the seating banks were lined with tiers of wooden seats, while the upper tiers were enclosed within an open-framed grandstand probably made of wood. In all, the amphitheatre held 6,000 spectators. Access to the seats was through passageways, while the upper tiers were reached by staircases with arched doorways. It was a massive structure enclosed within an external wall reaching thirty-two feet high. It also had an outer retaining wall measuring five and a half feet thick with strongly built buttresses inside and out to strengthen the structure even further. These heavily reinforced walls have survived, including many of the gateways leading into the arena. In all, the spectacle makes a visit here worthwhile. It can also be seen that stones from the wall separating the spectators from the arena have been extensively robbed in the past.

There were eight entrances in all, spaced evenly around the arena, two of which were for special processions only. There were also specially brick-built 'holding areas' where animals and gladiators waited before entering the arena.

The arena itself had first been covered with fine sand to a depth of two feet, then it was covered over with large pebbles obtained from the riverbed. But when the amphitheatre fell into decay around the second half of the third century, the buttresses had to be rebuilt and the arena was surfaced with gravel, broken bricks and stone slabs, which were the only materials available at the time. During the 1927 excavations, Mortimer Wheeler found that during these latest repairs, the 290-foot-long drain, which had run from the main north entrance straight down the middle to discharge excess rainwater directly into the river, had been partially filled up with sand into which a glass beaker, a gaming disc and a handled jug had found their way. After being cleared, the drain functioned as well as it had all those centuries ago. The glass beaker was said to have been produced by the glass factories of the Rhine during the first century, and had been engraved with a scene of a chariot race. Other interesting finds were two beautifully enamelled pendants dated to the third century, one of which had a pattern on both sides. Reproductions of these have been on sale at the Legionary Museum.

At the amphitheatre several stone inscriptions were discovered that had been built into the arena wall. These recorded that the rebuilding work had been carried out by the Second Augustan Legion. Bricks stamped LEG II AVG ANTO had been used to repair the walls. The addition of 'ANTO' into the legion's logo represented the name of the Emperor Antoninius, who had bestowed this high honour on the legion for its distinguished services. When all the repairs had been concluded, the amphitheatre continued in use until the end of the third century, as indicated by the discovery of nineteen coins from AD 254–296, recovered from the repaired road surfaces. But afterwards the structure fell into irreversible decay and, just like its neighbours, it became a quarry for the ambitious medieval builder.

It is also apparent that the amphitheatre had suffered some destruction during the fourteenth century, as coins dating from the reigns of Edward I and II were found there, no doubt having been lost by the vandals. Even fifty coins from the reigns of George I and II implied that stone robbing was still active at the site during the eighteenth century.

Although the grassed arena and the grass mounds are the only remains left, the entire site has a magical charm that adds to its tranquillity, and it is a popular venue for picnics. Just sitting with a lunchtime sandwich while admiring the glorious scenery of green-shrouded hills is a treat in itself.

## The Harbour Excavations between 2007 and 2010

Since a large part of the town still remained to be discovered in 2006, a series of excavations have been carried out since then. A year later, students from the University of Wales, Cardiff, under the direction of Dr Peter Guest, undertook as part of their archaeological project the task of making further excavations to discover what lay hidden beneath the unexplored pastures, and began excavating in the Prysg Field area next to the amphitheatre. After completing only one session of trial excavations in 2007, they came across a very large building thought to have been a warehouse. Then during the summers of 2008 to 2010, excavations in the area revealed many items of armour that reflected the personal tastes of the legionaries who had worn them. One legionary had fitted an unusual buckle made of bronze with a lattice design to his belt, and another had a custom-made ornamental top fitted over the pommel of his sword. One had also lost an iron finger ring set with a red carnelian carved with a figure, probably of the patron of good fortune to bring him luck. Other soldiers may also have worn this type of ring.

Continuing their examination of the area, the students made a geophysical study which revealed an area that was not thought to have been occupied in the Roman era, and they were surprised to see that outlines of enormous buildings were lying between the amphitheatre and the River Usk. In the five years leading up to these excavations, eight previously unknown barrack blocks have been found along with three large granaries, a monumental metal workshop and large store buildings.

Then, in addition to these discoveries, the ongoing excavations of 2010 surprised the world again, revealing that *Isca* had yet another large 'forgotten' suburb by the banks of the Usk. Administrative buildings, a market place, probably the forum, more houses and temples were all found. In consequence, the discoveries led to the most surprising revelation of all, that *Isca Silurum* once had an extensive harbour on the banks of the Usk. The remains were said to have been well preserved and included the main quay, landing stages and wharfs. This latter discovery exceeded all the university's expectations and was regarded as a major discovery. Its immense size clearly intimated that the fortress had been intended to become a major administrative centre in western Roman Britain, and that *Isca* had become a major port in this part of Roman Wales, capable of handling a large volume of ships that brought in goods from the Continent. To emphasise its importance, the port is only the second to have been discovered and excavated in Roman Britain after the one in London. Its discovery was also said to have been of great national importance as it propelled Caerleon to become one of the major Roman sites in Europe, and ranks as having the largest complex of buildings both in Roman Britain and Europe.

As was expected, the excavations generated enormous interest. The discovery of the port was announced in a BBC news bulletin, and during the last week of excavations in the period of 30 to 31 August, 2011, some 5,000 spectators arrived to watch the excavations. Over 400 were said to have followed progress on Twitter, and 250 on Facebook.

Following these momentous discoveries, the University of Wales was nominated for the annual Current Archaeological Award, 2013, for outstanding contributions to archaeology for that year.

By the fourth century the Roman town of *Isca* started to disintegrate, and its final demise occurred when it was finally burnt to the ground by Llewelyn the Great in 1231, after which, when a new town emerged, it was built over the top of the Roman remains.

In the early days of Christianity, Caerleon was the See of St Dubritius, the predecessor of St David, and had been inhabited by Welsh princes. Even in the following centuries Caerleon continued to attract visitors; in the thirteenth century, Gerald Cambrensis, known as 'Gerald of Wales', described the ruined fortress as 'being an imposing ruin on the landscape'. Among its other notable visitors were members of a French expeditionary force who, having been recruited to support Owain Glyndwr in 1405, took time off to visit the ruins. Even Lord Tennyson found the town inspiring enough to write some of his poems while staying there.

For motorists, Caerleon is accessible from the M4 motorway and is well signposted from the eastbound junction 26 before reaching Newport, and it can be reached by leaving junction 25 at the westbound junction. For those depending on public transport, a regular bus service leaves Newport every fifteen minutes each day and will stop immediately outside the Legionary Museum, which is in a central position for visiting the Fortress Baths, the Amphitheatre and the Barrack Blocks. There are also many bed-and-breakfast establishments, including some well-appointed hotels.

# 2

# *Venta Silurum*: Caerwent

Modern Caerwent lies ten miles to the east of Caerleon, between Newport and Chepstow, and occupies a central position along the South Wales coastal plain. In pre-Roman days, it was a market town surrounded by rich agricultural land, and when the Romans took control they named it *Venta Silurum*, which translates to 'Market Place of the Silures'.

The Romans did not build a military station here, but, because it had access to the sea via its tidal river, they did find its location helpful in ferrying supplies to fortresses around the coast. As the cost of supplying the army had become a drain on their resources, the Romans decided to reduce the number of men they had based at their fortresses, and as the size of the fortresses diminished, they began to concentrate on relations with the natives themselves, so that in being more moderate towards the natives and introducing them to Roman ways, the Romans created a more peaceful environment that did not need such a strong military presence. Therefore, with the reduction in military power and a more moderate approach from the Romans, there followed an era where the natives became masters of their own destinies. It was in this environment that the inhabitants of *Venta* were given the status of self-government, so they could make their own laws and collect taxes, albeit under strict supervision. It also took the responsibility of administration costs off the Romans. More importantly, *Venta Silurum* became the tribal capital of the Silures, and was the largest centre of civilian population in Roman Wales. It was in this encouraging environment that the town prospered. There is evidence that it was still an active community in the fourth century, with all the attendant luxuries of having classical architecture and a high standard of living. From the examination of coins, pottery, glass and metalwork it is thought that the town had been established around AD 74/75, only a few years after the conquest of South Wales had been achieved by the legionary forces.

At the time of its foundation, all the internal buildings had been of timber, but as building techniques progressed, the timber houses were soon replaced with stone-built ones. In pre-Roman days, most of the Silurian settlements and hill forts had been defended by deep ditches and palisades, but the new inhabitants of *Venta Silurum* did not have any. During the second century, however, they must have thought that one was necessary, as an earthen rampart was created on a cobbled surface as wide as thirty feet and as high as six feet. This was later modified by building a high stone wall in front of the rampart, which surrounded the town in an almost elongated square with rounded corners. They had been massively built to a thickness of seven or eight feet, and rose to an average height of nine feet, in places rising to seventeen feet high. *Venta* is said to have the best-preserved defences of any Roman town in Britain, with a circuit exceeding one mile long. The northern and southern walls were something over 500 yards long, and those in the east and west were about 390 yards long. In modern times, the north wall was found to have bowed outwards, probably due to ground subsidence, but the southern wall was nearly straight and had maintained its full height of seventeen feet.

14. The East Wall.

The walls had a gate at each point of the compass and these were later flanked by towers. The walls eventually replaced the ramparts and had a total length of 1,280 feet. In Roman times, the west and east gates were the principal entrances into the town, through which the Roman road ran. The Roman road is still there, serving the traffic entering the present-day village from Newport via the west gate. However, the north and south walls, which had allowed light traffic to enter the town, were later walled up, probably when the roads were no longer used.

The south wall was known locally as the Port Wall, as there had once been a river flowing nearby which had carried boats right up to the walls of the town. Large iron rings attached to the walls indicate that was where the boats had been tied.

*Venta* had developed a street system dividing the town into twenty equally sized *insulae* (plots), with two rows of five on either side of the main road, which effectively divided the town into two halves. Four streets ran north to south and were intersected by three streets running east to west. Some of the roads were surprisingly narrow and must have carried only light traffic. One of these was Pound Lane, which ran north-westwards off the main road to reach the north gate. Back in Roman times, they had been the responsibility of the local council and were surfaced with rammed gravel, with cambered sides for draining away excess rain water.

As bathing was an essential element in Roman daily life, there was a separate building for communal bathing, but the fact that many of the houses had their own bathing suites suggested that *Venta*'s population had become very affluent to have afforded this in their own homes. As the fortunes of the people of *Venta* improved, it attracted successful merchants and other wealthy people from the neighbouring areas to settle in the town. It even attracted retired soldiers from the Second Augustan Legion to settle there. As the land surrounding the town was prime agricultural land with good grazing, it was an ideal place to raise cattle and sustain a good lifestyle.

Although the walls had begun to disintegrate and were robbed of their stone over the centuries, they still made a powerful statement on the landscape, and as the centuries passed by, just like with the amphitheatre at Caerleon, no one knew they were Roman. Even when the Elizabethan antiquary John Leyland visited the site in 1540, he only found a few newly built farm cottages within the walls. It was recorded, though, that tessellated pavements unique to the Roman period had been found in both 1777 and 1830, some of which were wantonly destroyed. And it was not until 1855 that local antiquary Octavius Morgan decided to investigate the reported Roman remains.

He began excavations after a trial exploration in the south-west corner of the town in 1899, when he found a bathhouse. The work was instigated by the Clifton Antiquarian Club of Bristol, who had arranged excursions for the study of archaeological objects in the West Country and South Wales. Excavations continued until 1913 and were mainly conducted by men from the town working with only picks and shovels. A great deal of progress was made and by the end of 1913 nearly two-thirds of the town had been excavated. Two world wars then appear to have halted further exploration, but they started again after the Second World War in 1946. In modern times, the excavations were given numbers for identification purposes.

As *Venta* had not been built over like Caerleon, it was possible to find the complete foundations of many buildings, including private residences, the basilica-forum and two temples, from which it could be determined that *Venta Silurum* had indeed been a town of some influence and beauty, with an affluent society, its own judiciary and a tribal council.

Many of the properties at *Venta* reflected the social status of the owners. The houses of the rich were larger and usually their rooms were arranged around a central courtyard, which brought in extra daylight. They were lavishly decorated with coloured plaster walls and mosaic floors. The houses of the poor were simple. Their rooms were smaller with tessellated floors. Some of them served as shops or workshops opening directly on to the road for trading. Over time, even these simple dwellings evolved into larger and more luxurious homes as the family prospered, as the excavations were soon to prove.

## Plots II – IV

Many buildings of various sizes were found in these plots, including a large area thought to have been the town's cattle market, but they could not be exposed.

15. Caerwent village centre with the war memorial.

## Plot V, House 22N

This was the last plot in the north-western part of the town, and two large buildings were noted lying down its eastern side, one of which was another large house with multiple rooms surrounding a central courtyard. But it was house 22N, in the north-east corner, which attracted the most attention. It contained eleven rooms and was quite unlike any other building so far excavated. It had a frontage of 110 feet, and the northern rooms had been altered to include a nave, along with an east-facing apse and a vestibule, which suggested they had been used for Christian worship. Room 1 had a pavement of rough stone slabs, while Room 2 had a concrete floor three feet above the grass, suggesting that it had been elevated. Among the foundations were numerous white and blue limestone and red-brick *tesserae*, which had covered the floor of the apse. Coins of Tetricus I, Augusta, and Constantinus II that were found in the room dated it to the middle of the third century.

## Plot VI

The partial foundations of a long building were found extending lengthways along the main road, but they were not left exposed.

## Plot VII, Courtyard House 26N

These excavations, located in Pound Lane, are the first to be seen after leaving the car park and are immediately visible from the main road, with Pound Lane leading off from it on the left.

Excavations here revealed the existence of two narrow strip buildings, which had been built side by side and had occupied the south-west corner of this plot since the middle of the second century. The two buildings had been separated by a narrow gap, now outlined as a long strip of grass. But they were not the first to have occupied this site. The foundations confirm that a timber structure had occupied the site along with a kiln for producing pottery, and had probably been occupied by the very first settlers.

Originally, each building had possessed living quarters in the rear with a workshop at the front of the house with simple concrete floors, although their walls had been given better attention with coloured plaster.

The foundations reveal that the building on the right-hand side had undergone several alterations during its long history to make it into one large building a century later. The most noticeable feature is the thickness and sturdiness of the outside walls.

The discovery of lumps of slag and hearths confirmed that blacksmithing had taken place in the workshop of the building on the right-hand side. It appears that as the years went by, the owner had saved enough money to buy his neighbour's property next door, which he then demolished in order to enlarge his own property. He also enlarged the workshop and equipped it with a new forge. However, the extensions into his neighbour's

16. The strip buildings along Pound Lane.

old property could not be excavated because they lie beneath the adjoining gardens, and it is impossible to know what trade had been carried on there before it was acquired by the blacksmith. Therefore only the extensions on the right-hand side and facing Pound Lane could be fully exposed after excavation.

As the blacksmith continued to prosper from the patronage of his customers, he altered his living quarters yet again to install two mosaic floors in the rooms, as well as splitting the workshop into two to make a small addition in the north-east corner in the form of a store room. Interestingly, the excavators found two nearly complete storage jars, and an ingot of lead that had been stamped LEG II AVG and had obviously found its way there from the legionary workshops at Caerleon. With the building of a new wing, the building grew to extend around three sides of a courtyard. The front of the house was improved with a covered footpath, and a portico was paved with flagstones, the roof of which was supported by columns. This created an impressive entrance. They also made a door into Pound Lane. This is now marked by a flat piece of stone, clearly visible, which was used to support the door jambs. Red tiles had originally covered the roof, but these were exchanged for hexagonal stone slabs which, according to the rubble found on site, had been cut on the premises.

The house was still occupied in the fifth century, as indicated by the hoard of 150 coins dating to around AD 425 found lying among the rubbish of the room that was used for smelting iron. It was possible that the coins had fallen from where they had been hidden in the loft when the floors fell in after the house fell into ruin.

This interesting house stretches along the right side of Pound Lane and is open to the public.

## Plot VII, Courtyard House 27N

This interesting house lies to the rear of the last mentioned property, and was separated only by a very short gap. From outward appearances, this house looks as though it was a continuation of the last one, as both dwellings occupied almost the entire length of Pound Lane.

Among the house's features were two wings and a central courtyard, now marked by a rectangular patch of grass. Only two wings of this property could be excavated, but walking among the foundations gives a good idea as to the size of the rooms.

The south wing, extending across the whole site, had five rooms, but only four could be partially exposed as they too lie beneath gardens. Above the wing there was a large courtyard. It had been paved with flagstones, but only a very small portion could be excavated.

The rest of the property, called the west wing, followed the line of Pound Lane and also had five rooms. But they were much smaller than those in the south, and had been laid with yellow coloured concrete. One room in the north-west adjoining Pound Lane possessed a mosaic floor that had been heated by a hypocaust. Although the sandstone pillars supporting the floor were still in their original places, the furnace could not be found. The mosaic itself had an attractive pattern in red and grey showing dolphins inside circles as part of a large square design. In the centre was a picture of a *cantharus* – a drinking vessel also used for mixing wine – which had originated from Greece. Adding to this were the colours of the painted wall plaster. There is a possibility that the house had an upper storey, as there is a small space between two rooms of that wing which could have accommodated a staircase, but it was not found. The roof had been covered with stone slabs.

Above the courtyard was a walled enclosure, which was thought to have been a small walled garden. These were popular in Roman times, especially to the rich, who were inclined to use them as formal areas for relaxing out of doors. The gardens, usually containing shrubs, were set out in geometric designs, but the garden here may have been a kitchen garden where the householder preferred to grow the new produce which had arrived from the Mediterranean, like lettuce, cucumber, cabbage, peas and pumpkins, and several hundred varieties of herbs, including rosemary. At that time, tomatoes and potatoes were non-existent. Potatoes did not arrive from North America until the late sixteenth century during the reign of Elizabeth I. Neither could the Roman housewife eat fruit such as oranges, grapefruit or apricots. They were introduced by the Arabs during the Middle Ages. But lemons were plentiful; they were produced around the Mediterranean and probably shipped to Britain with the rest of the new produce. Bee keeping was also a popular pursuit. After all, it produced honey, which was the only ingredient available to sweeten dishes, as sugar was not available – it would eventually come from the Caribbean in the sixteenth century. The only drinks available were milk and wine. The latter was imported from the Mediterranean in *amphorae*. These earthenware vessels had elongated shapes that sometimes came to a point at the end, and were designed to stack easily into the ships bringing them to Britain. They also contained olive oil – another new ingredient, imported from Spain, with which the Roman housewife cooked and filled terracotta lamps in order to light her home. Olive oil was also used to cleanse the body in the absence of soap – another commodity not available in Roman times. The *amphorae* carrying the olive oil were broken up and not used again after they had become empty because their interiors had soaked up the oil to such an extent that they turned rancid and gave off a foul smell. Another popular way of flavouring dishes was with a fish sauce, but it too gave off a foul smell while being prepared, and was literally banned in built-up areas. However, it had a pleasant taste when eaten. In this rural environment perhaps our housewife here had no such problems with neighbours' complaints.

The walled garden marked the northern end of the house. It also marked the top end of Pound Lane.

## Courtyard House 28N

This enormous establishment is located just a few paces to the north-west of the last house, and is situated in its own little exclusive area off Pound Lane in Plot I, which was accessible from Plot VII where the courtyard houses had been situated. This very large house had been built over a previous property that was demolished in the late second century to make way for the present one.

Excavations were carried out in 1981 and 1984 when it was revealed that this courtyard house had also been built to a very high standard and contained as many as sixteen

17. Underfloor channel to direct heat into the room.

rooms arranged around two courtyards, one enclosing ten rooms in the southern part of the property and the other enclosing six rooms at its northern end, where only two of the four rooms at its northern end could be fully exposed. The one on the western side did not reveal itself, and only half of the other end room on the far-eastern side could be excavated. In fact, the entire eastern section of this building could not be excavated at all as it lay beneath the adjoining property; the tall hedge of the adjoining garden acted as a kind of boundary between the two properties. Those rooms to the west of the courtyard were fully excavated, and one at its southern end had a hypocaust. The sandstone pillars that had supported the floor have survived.

The rooms around the northern courtyard had their walls and ceilings lavishly decorated and may have served as the family's living quarters. A fine mosaic pavement was found in the corridor leading off from the courtyard. This had a large blue Greek 'key' design set against a background of white tiles and was removed to the National Museum of Wales. The room that had been fully excavated in the northern range possessed a hypocaust, and its supporting pillars also survived, as did the furnace. This room was by far the largest and may have been the family's dining room.

In comparison, the rooms around the southern courtyard were more modest with tessellated floors and may have had more domestic functions such as that of kitchen, larder and storeroom, and perhaps provided quarters for the servants. One room here, though, had been given the benefit of a hypocaust. Another room had its floors raised

18. Courtyard house (28N) off Pound Lane.

and was probably used for storing grain. Its raised floor would have kept out rodents and would have allowed air to circulate to prevent the grain from getting mouldy.

It is thought that this enormous dwelling may have been a farmhouse. There was certainly enough land to the west of the property for cultivation or for an orchard. There were a small number of outbuildings in the vicinity which may have been barns and cow sheds.

In Roman times, work on the land was the principal employment for many of the citizens. This included the production of food and keeping livestock – cattle for meat and hides and sheep for the supply of wool for the woven garments which were still generally worn. At this time, horses were not used for heavy agricultural duties as a harness suitable for the animal to pull heavy loads without being strangled had not been devised. Horses were only used for lighter duties such as pulling carts with lighter loads, or ceremonial or racing chariots. The heavier work was carried out by oxen. The Romans had good farming tools that were not unlike those used today, such as scythes, sickles, spades, forks and axes. They were even known to have had a wheeled plough, which was Gallic in origin, and a threshing machine with spiked axles that originated in Carthaginia.

In this rural setting, many of the townspeople would have been engaged in agriculture, where wool, beef and hides were the principal products, and the surrounding farmland would have accommodated the cottages for the farm workers.

19. The hypocaust pillars of the dining room of House 28N.

This enormous house was occupied until the second half of the fourth century, when it was abandoned and gradually fell into ruin just like its neighbours. A lane behind the property to the west of this courtyard house leads the visitor back to the main road and the war memorial.

## The Romano-Celtic Temple: Plot IX

This was a significant discovery since not many temples of this era have so far been found. It was located immediately behind the stone wall leading into the village a short distance from Pound Lane, and to the west of the houses in Pound Lane. It is the next excavation to be seen along the main road leading into the village. A gap in the wall leads the visitor inside.

It was first excavated in 1909, then again between 1984 and 1991, and lay in the south-west corner of Plot IX. There were other buildings to its west and north, and although these were mapped, they could not be exposed for viewing. The temple was thought to have been built during the earlier part of the second century, and remained in use until the late third century.

Upon entering the site, the first part of the temple to be seen is its long corridor, which runs east to west and used to lie inside a raised portico, entered by a small flight of steps. This portico, which was probably made of timber, has disappeared. There was a door in the centre of the corridor which gave access to a long hall leading towards the inner sanctuaries. The hall had been elaborately decorated, with columns built against the walls, and would have made another impressive entry into the sanctuaries, which were contained in two square enclosures, one inside the other, with the innermost one being the sacred shrine.

The shrine contained the sacred statue of the deity being worshipped, but it was not known who the deity was. Not many people would have had access to it, and the worshippers would have stood in the sacred grounds to watch the ceremonies. The shrine was surrounded by an ambulatory around which the worshippers could walk. In fact, the whole of the inner temple was enclosed by wide walkways where worshippers would gather. These also provided shelter for the ritual processions. A nearby rubbish pit turned up some interesting finds. They included a small squat sandstone carving of a seated woman representing a mother goddess holding a fruit and a small tree – the symbols of fertility. It may have been one of the deities within the shrine. The other find was an iron finger ring with the face of a child, and a small circular boss with the face of Medusa which may have been a decoration from a wooden box containing a ritual object. Iron finger rings were worn generally by both men and women.

20. The Romano-Celtic temple showing the inner shrine and apse.

*Above:* 21. The Romano-Celtic temple showing the long entrance hall and passage leading left to the inner shrine.

*Right:* 22. Mother Goddess found near the Romano-Celtic Temple.

## Plot IX, 7N

In this same plot and to the north of the temple, but not exposed for public viewing, was a large residence with multiple rooms, numbered 7N. It was excavated in 1907 and found to have had a rectangular courtyard in its centre, with six rooms at its southern end. However, only a few of the rooms in the northern part of the house could be excavated. Interestingly, a number of vessels were found sealed inside an urn, which had been buried in the fourth-century levels of the house. One of these was a pewter bowl whose base had been scratched with Christian symbols comprising the first two Greek letters of Christ's name. This action of hiding the bowl inside an urn and then burying it suggested that the family had tried to hide their Christianity, particularly if they thought they were in some danger at that time. This bowl may have been part of an early Christian supper known as the *agape* (friendly affection) given secretly at the house. These suppers were given after the Eucharist by some well-to-do members of the community for his poorer neighbours. There was no evidence of a purposely built chapel inside the house, but Christian worship in Roman times did take place within the home.

## The Forum-Basilica: Plot VIII

This was another significant discovery. The basilica and its forum occupy the entire area of Plot VIII, and lie to the west of the temple, but only the basilica could be excavated. As it occupies the northern part of the plot and lies behind an existing farm, which is occupying the southern half, it is not visible from the road. The farm is located on the area the forum had once occupied. Access to the basilica's excavations is by proceeding through the clump of trees at the northern end of the temple and veering to the east for a few yards.

   The site was first explored in 1908 and 1909, but a later examination of the plot soon revealed the structural history of the basilica. It was found that its outside walls had been painted off-white. Entrance was by way of a monumental archway on its eastern side, the foundations for which are clearly visible to the visitor today. Only its northern rooms and western areas could be excavated and exposed for public viewing. In one of the northern rooms was the prestigious council chamber, where all the debates and important decisions in the town's administration were heard. Its layout can be clearly seen, as well as the channels that had been cut into its floor to make way for the wooden benches on which the councillors sat. It was the largest room in the basilica, and with its walls decorated with coloured plaster and two magnificent mosaics covering the floor, it was a room to be admired. One of the mosaics lay by the entrance, the other one lying at right angles down the middle of the room to form a 'T' shape together. Unfortunately the mosaics had disappeared by the time the basilica was found. Only fragments of their borders survived. This destruction probably occurred when the basilica underwent several alterations in the late third century. An interesting discovery was that of the stone bases of a stepped wooden dais from which

23. The forum/basilica. To the right is the furnace of the hypocaust that obstructed the entrance, and to the right is the hot snack shop of the forum with the foundations of its furnace in the top-left-hand corner.

24. The two broad aisles of the basilica.

the magistrates would have presided. This feature was unique to *Venta*, as it has not been observed anywhere else in Roman Britain. The rear wall of the council chamber was still standing to a height of six feet at excavation and had been incorporated into the adjoining wall of the farm buildings. It had been lavishly decorated with artwork in coloured plaster, but this mural was removed only recently and taken away for preservation. Next to the council chamber is the shrine. This room was used for prayers, and contained a bust of the emperor and the local deity. The other rooms were used as offices.

Below the northern rooms was the north aisle. It and the south aisle lay on either side of the great hall, which stretched across the building from east to west. The great hall would have been used for large public meetings and ceremonies. The aisles were separated by colonnades of Corinthian columns which reached a height of thirty feet, and the walls which had carried the columns were massive, with foundations to a depth of six feet. The roof was also high, reaching sixty-five feet, so the entire building would have towered over the town. Windows were arranged around the roof area in a similar way to later cathedrals, whose designs were inspired by these great structures. On either side of the great hall was a room for the tribunal, where the magistrates heard civil cases. The eastern one showed that in the later years it required heating, so its pillars and furnace were the only remnants left of the room. Being the end room, the furnace was located on its outside walls, but it tended to obstruct the entrance into the basilica. The slabs of the furnace can be seen just inside the excavated entrance.

Excavations also revealed the box drain beneath the basilica which carried away excess rainwater from the gutters. Although the drain was covered and lined with massive sandstone slabs weighing as much as one ton, it had been paved with tiles. A hole cut into one of the blocks which had lain under the south aisle suggested that a water feature had been there, as the water had terminated at that point. After passing under the basilica, the drain then ran northwards and into a yard where it discharged into a soakaway.

In the late third century the basilica underwent major alterations. The roof of the great hall had been stripped, and the columns dismantled. Certain walls were strengthened and the floors were raised, probably because of subsidence or the timbers had rotted. Meanwhile, the building continued to function until the 340s, confirmed by the discovery of coins of that period. But the use of the building appeared to change; the floors of the great hall were removed and hearths appeared, suggesting that the hall had been used for metal working. Coins dated to the 390s suggested that some of the rooms may have functioned up until then, but there was no evidence to suggest they had continued for very much longer, as the entire building was systematically destroyed and the site levelled. The only remnants of this once majestic building were the foundations and the other small structural items left on site, including the distinctive capitals of the magnificent Corinthian columns, which were taken to the Newport Museum.

## The Forum: Plot VIII

The forum, meaning market place, was a large open space that was part of the basilica's southern approaches and comprised an enormous piazza surrounded by shops and offices. The piazza would have been busy on market days when traders would have set up temporary stalls. As such, the forum also played an important role in the life of the inhabitants, and was the hub of the community.

But as the land was occupied by an existing farm, the only part of the forum that could be excavated was the one shop situated in the north-western corner, lying against the basilica's entrance. The shop was thought to have been a snack bar selling hot food, as a stone hearth was found in one corner. Gaming counters and personal items such as tweezers, nail cleaners and ear scrapers were found among the rubble inside the shop and may have fallen through the wooden floorboards. Beyond, the only other walls found were the two from the second shop, and part of the inner walls of the long promenade which ran southwards down the length of the shops. In keeping with the usual design, the

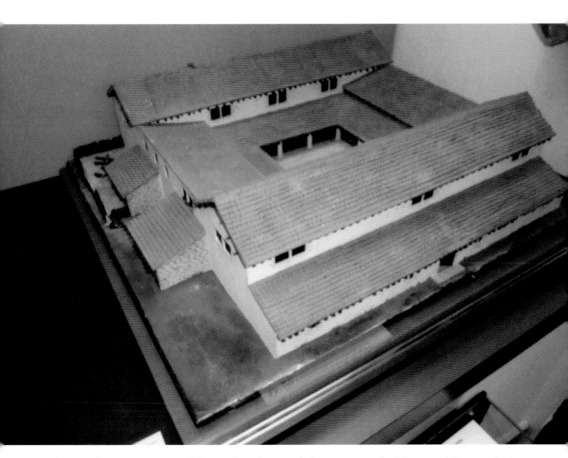

25. A typical Roman courtyard house found around Caerwent, at the Newport Museum & Art Gallery.

roofs covering the promenades would have been supported by tall columns. The forum extended to reach the main road, where its entrance had probably been. The trees of the existing farmhouse that prevented the full excavation of the forum can be clearly seen in the temple's photograph.

## Plot X

This was the last *insula* situated on the northern half of the town, but no Roman buildings of any kind were found there.

It was then left to the archaeologists to investigate plots XI–XX in the southern part of the town on the other side of the main road. And, although a substantial number of very large Roman homes and buildings such as the civic baths were found in various parts of this southern section, all the excavations had to be covered up and the land returned to its original state, thereby leaving nothing to be seen of the Roman period above ground. Where it was not possible to excavate, geophysical surveys and ground-penetrating radar were used, which greatly helped in providing detailed information about the layouts of the individual buildings within and beyond the limits of the town. However, some documentation was made, and these are as follows.

## Plot XI, House 7S

This particular plot was the first of the southern section to be excavated and was fully occupied with Roman buildings, the first of which was the house numbered 7S. Its foundations indicated that it also possessed a very large central courtyard with multiple rooms around three of its sides. There was also an extension to the right-hand side of the property which contained longer rooms, and an extension to its southern part. And just when it was thought that there were no more surprises to be found, this house turned up trumps with a complete mosaic still in its original place in the family's dining room, which was considered another major find. The mosaic, containing thousands of light blue and pale grey tesserae with red, yellow and white strands, was revealed to be a gigantic pattern in excess of twenty-one feet by thirty-four feet overall, and comprised a nine-panel design of geometric patterns of squares inside circles with animals, said to be hounds, in the centre of each pattern and a human head at each corner. These heads were interpreted as representing the four seasons; the head that appeared to be wearing a red topknot or Phrygian cap with a purple-brown cloak around her shoulders was named 'Winter', and working clockwise, the next figure, with short hair and a red flower on her chest, was named 'Spring'. The figure which was thought to have represented autumn was lost. Unfortunately only a small section of the central octagon survived, and there was no way of knowing what the figure there had been. The mosaic was made more interesting by the appearance of the four encircled cupids on either side of the central octagon. They had feathery wings and appeared to be carrying torches with red tesserae as flames. The mosaic was hailed as a great find and was the only one

26. A section of the four seasons mosaic found in House 7S in Plot XI.

of this size to have survived. It was carefully removed from the site and taken to the Newport Museum, where it has remained on public display.

## House 15S

This was another interesting house lying to the east of the last property, and was even larger, with multiple rooms around two courtyards. The house possessed another mosaic pavement, but the main discovery here was that the house had a cellar in which was the only surviving window to be found in Venta. As it was the cellar, the window openings were fairly large, and the window glass, like all Roman window glass, had a blue-green tint and was not completely transparent.

Roman town houses usually had wooden shutters or iron grilles to protect their openings, so window glass was an interesting discovery. Glass objects like drinking glasses and vases, etc., arrived from the factories of northern Gaul, the Rhineland, and from Italy. Glass for the specific use of windows was known to have been blown locally.

27. Discovery of four seasons mosaic during early excavations.

It was made from sand, soda and lime. The natural content of the sand gave rise to the blue-green colour, but manganese was used to make the glass clear. A range of colours in the glass could also be produced by the addition of various metal oxides. Items such as vases were usually made from moulds. The Romans also used glass containers to store the cremated remains of their loved ones. Specimens of these are displayed at the Caerleon Legionary Museum.

## Plot XII, House 16S

This house occupied the adjoining plot, and was one of the two large properties found there. They were lying so close together that they looked like one enormous property and occupied the entire northern end of the plot.

A surprising discovery was made in House 16 when one room produced a large portion of bone, which turned out to be from a whale. Other parts of the whale's skeleton were found in another part of the house. Why they were there remains a mystery, but it was certainly a surprising discovery to the excavators while they were sifting for items among the foundations.

The most historic find in this house, however, was a stone altar with a Latin inscription reading, 'To the god Mars-Ocelus, Aelius Augustinus, *optio*, willingly and deservedly fulfils his vow.' An *optio* was a sub-centurion, and whatever favour Augustinus had asked the god, he had repaid him with some kind of offering. The Roman god Mars was a national divinity and was originally associated with agriculture, but the Romans made him god of war by adopting him as a symbol during their various campaigns. Ocelus was the Celtic equivalent and they were usually mentioned together.

There are also several narrow strip buildings occupying this plot. They are located in its northern end and lie at right angles to the main road, just like those in Pound Lane. They were residences with shops attached, separated by a narrow passage. There were also some shops, and two blocks had shared a common portico.

28. An altar dedicated to Mars and Ocelus, found in House 16S, Plot XII, now in St Stephen's church.

## Plot XIII

Shops were located here next to the main road and had been attached to their owners' premises. But the main discovery here were the civic baths, which lay opposite the shops and were in a prime location to be entered from the main road. From the layout of the plan, the hypocausts of the three main pools were located, but only part of the southern area could be excavated.

The present church of St Stephens is also located in this plot, and thirty skeletons were found in the vicarage orchard. One skeleton had been buried in a coffin of red sandstone blocks, which had probably come from one of the floors of the nearby houses.

To the south of the plot and built up against the southern defence wall was another enormous building containing multiple rooms, a courtyard and a wide corridor on the west. The layout was interpreted as belonging to another *mansio* or guest house.

## Plots XIV and XV

No Roman buildings were located.

## Plot XVI

This plot was occupied by a building of enormous proportions with a double row of rooms arranged around a large central courtyard. Its floor plan showed that it had been extensively enlarged on its western side to give the appearance of two large buildings. This house, numbered 2S, could only have belonged to a wealthy family who had lavishly decorated it with wall paintings, one fragment of which was uncovered at excavation. It was a young woman's face with well-defined features. It had been beautifully painted and showed her wearing the short curly hair that was typically Roman in style. Another fragment showed just an arm, maybe of the same girl, with the hand holding a sprig of flowers.

This very valuable fragment showing Roman art at its very best is now on display at the Newport Museum. This discovery makes one wonder if the rest of the house had been just as beautiful. It also makes one wonder how many wall paintings had eluded the excavators in Venta alone because they had been destroyed in antiquity. No one will ever know, but after seeing the one in House 2S it would be safe to say that had they survived, they would have equalled those seen in Pompeii.

To the south of the above house was another dwelling, numbered 3S, but only the central courtyard and its surrounding set of rooms could be excavated. A wall extended from the house towards the west to connect with two rooms, but they may have been outbuildings.

## Plot XVII

The outline of the buildings here were very fragmented, and it was not possible to get a clear outline of a complete building, although there appeared to be a house with long

29. Segment of a portrait of a young woman on wall plaster in House 2S, Plot XVI.

corridors extending southwards. The northern section of this plot was also well occupied, but only partial foundations could be seen.

## Plot XVIII

Three extremely large buildings fully occupied this plot. The one in the north-west corner was not so well defined. The second building was located in the middle of the plot and was numbered 11S. The most interesting discovery at this house was the base of a statue with a Latin inscription that was translated as:

> To the god Mars-Lenus, otherwise known as Ocelus Vellaunus, and to the divinity of the Emperor Marcus Nonius Romanus presented this at his own expense in recognition of the immunity from tax granted to his guild. On the tenth day of the Kalends of September, in the consulship of Glabrio and Homulus.

Mars-Lenus was a Rheinish god from the district of Trier and had probably been introduced to Venta by the legionaries who had retired there from Caerleon, or by traders visiting from the Continent. Ocelus Vellaunus – meaning 'the powerful' – was a local deity and was associated with Mars. On top of the pedestal were traces of the deity's feet as well as a sacred bird. Reference to the Emperor revealed a connection with Rome. It created a sense of unity among Roman exiles throughout the Empire. The stone base in now at the Newport Museum.

To the south of House 11S there was another extremely large building alongside the southern defences that was numbered 12S. It also had multiple rooms around a courtyard, with a wide corridor dividing the rooms and another wide one on its western side. This layout suggested that the building could have been another guest house.

## Plots XIX and XX

These last two plots on the bottom row of the twenty *insulae* were at the far eastern end of the town, but apart from the baths, which were found astride these two plots, and a few isolated foundations in the north, no other buildings could be found. The baths, which were the first to be found by Octavius Morgan, were very small compared with the civic ones.

A circular temple was another discovery. It was located outside the town's defences on the left-hand side of the east gate and, judging from the circumference of its circular walls, it must have been an awe-inspiring sight that greatly impressed visitors entering by that gate.

Another discovery of historical significance was a large pedestal that had been the base for a statue carved out of Bath stone. It had been found in the centre of the village in a place now occupied by the war memorial since 1902. It was the only record found naming the town as *Civitas Silurum*. Called the 'Paulinus Inscription', it bore twelve lines of Latin associating Tiberius Claudius Paulinus, a former commandant of the Second Augustan Legion, with the town, probably in recognition of some kind act he had bestowed upon it. The Silures had erected the statue in his honour, and placed it in an honoured position in the centre of the town. Paulinus was commandant at Caerleon during Caracalla's reign, AD 211–17, and the pedestal records his career, which included the senatorial governorship of two Gallic provinces. It is one of the most important inscriptions to have been found in Roman Wales, as it recorded an act made by the tribal council of *Venta* on behalf of all the Silures. The stone now resides inside St Stephens Church.

Excavations of this magnitude collect a myriad of items from hundreds of pottery shards to small items which were once treasured possessions. Pottery was found in abundance on most Roman sites. As clay pots were relatively cheap and produced in mass quantities, they were easily discarded when broken. Most of the pottery for domestic use was manufactured in local kilns. So-called 'black burnished ware' was produced in Dorset, and another type was obtained from Oxfordshire – the so-called 'Oxford whites'. Pottery from the legionary kilns at Caerleon also found its way to Venta, as did some from nearby Caldicot, where there were six kilns in operation producing grey-coloured ware. The red-coloured Samian tableware was imported from the factories in northern Gaul and it arrived by the shipload. One ship carrying a load of Samian was sunk off the Kent coast in rough weather, and this has enabled modern divers to retrieve this distinctive pottery. Jewellery was another type of item found in large quantities around the town, *fibulae* (brooches) in particular. These were often decorated with patterns in coloured enamel, and were considered the height of fashion. Spinning whorls were also found in large numbers, which suggested that the ladies had continued with the tradition of spinning their own cloth at home. Personal keepsakes were also found in the form of tiny statuettes made from bone and bronze; favourites were those of animals and deities like Venus and Mars. Some spoons were also found. They were used to eat eggs, and their long spiky handles were used to pick snails out of their shells.

These are but a few of the items that were taken to the Newport Museum for public viewing. They enable us to look back to a time that has been lost.

The unexposed areas in the southern part of the town have been left for the next generation to investigate, and one wonders what else there is to find.

Non-motorists will find that buses to the village run from Newport each hour (opposite the railway station) via the service to Chepstow and will stop outside Pound Lane.

SAMIAN BOWL.
With the figure of a Triton
(a mythical sea creature)
From Caerwent. D2.5.225

SAMIAN BOWL WITH FIGURES OF
APOLLO PLAYING A LYRE,
PAN AND NEPTUNE
From Caerwent. D2.5.216

30. Two Samian bowls exhibited at the Newport Museum & Art Gallery.

# 3
# *Moridunum*: Carmarthen

In their sweep northward through Wales, the Roman army arrived in Demetae territory, next door to the Silures, around AD 74, and immediately established an auxiliary fortress here on the northern slopes of the Towy Valley which, for their purposes, commanded a strategic position and was only seven miles from the sea. As their preference was for being close to rivers, they sited it at the tidal limit of the River Towy.

The named their site *Moridunum* after the Celtic words 'Mori', meaning the sea, and 'dunum', meaning fortress. It was probably the natural features of the landscape that persuaded the Romans to station here, as it also had the advantage of being at the junction of three major roads, the Sarn Helen being one that led directly northwards to their other strategic fortress of *Segontium* (Caernarvon).

With the discovery in the town of a clay bank fronted by V-shaped ditches and a rampart strengthened by a palisade, it was thought to be possible that at the time of the Romans' arrival these had defended the ancient town, as most towns defended themselves in this way. However, with the arrival of the Roman army, the Demetae, like the Silures and the other tribes, had to concede defeat and accept Roman rule, especially the Roman way of life which they appear to have embraced.

While no one in Wales had known about the existence of the fortress or the civilian town here until the latter half of the twentieth century, the first-century Egyptian geographer Ptolemy was able to give its precise location, and correctly described the town as being the principal town of the Demetae. And in the twelfth century Geraldus Cambrensis (Gerald of Wales) described it in his travels: 'This ancient city is situated on the banks of the noble Tywy, surrounded by woods and pastures, and roughly enclosed with walls of brick, parts of which are still standing.' This gave a vivid description of as to how *Moridunum* looked in the twelfth century. The walls were mentioned again in the fourteenth-century *Cartulary of the Priory*, and even in the sixteenth century when Elizabethan antiquarian, William Camden, mentioned *Moridunum* in his *Britannia*, published in 1586.

In the nineteenth century, several tangible items of the Roman era surfaced when two altars were found, one of which was called the 'Nato Stone' due to its Latin inscription '*bono (o r) ei p(ublica) nato*', which was believed to have referred to a fourth-century Roman Emperor.

Further evidence of the Roman era surfaced when a tessellated floor, along with portions of an ancient wall, were found when a well was being dug in Priory Street. In 1897, what was believed to have been a Roman bathhouse also surfaced. A large amount of high-quality Samian tableware and a superb silver gilt brooch were also found.

As the finds continued into the twentieth century with the discovery of a pebbled roadway beneath demolished properties in Spillman Street in 1968 and the discovery of two more altars, one of which is now kept in the porch of St Peter's Church, they persuaded the authorities that serious excavations were in order to preserve whatever Roman remains lay beneath the ground.

The newly formed Dyfed Archaeological Trust took over this responsibility, and for the first time, there was a regionally based archaeological service to respond to the planned development in the town that threatened the Roman remains.

Many parts of the fortress were discovered, including its defences, main roads and barracks, but it was not possible to locate the principal buildings. In all, the fortress measured four to five acres and extended beyond the castle to lie beneath most of the modern buildings of the town. Although a full excavation could not be carried out, a wealth of pottery and a substantial amount of first-century Samian ware and coins were found throughout the site. However, a layer of burnt clay and charcoal above the original floors of the timber buildings suggested that the fortress had been purposely burnt down by the auxiliaries before they abandoned it around AD 150.

Sometime around this time, a planned street system had been laid out on the eastern side of the settlement, with further development taking place when numerous rectangular buildings were added. The town prospered well under the Romans, who then bestowed the title of *Moridunum Demetae* on it, thereby giving the inhabitants the right to govern themselves, just like the people of Caerwent.

The first sighting of the lost town of *Moridunum* came in 1968, when the foundations of four large buildings dated to the third century were discovered behind the north-west rampart of the fortress, suggesting that, like at Caerleon, a small community had also established itself there.

One building, considered residential, measured fifty-nine feet overall and had been divided into two rooms of twenty-six feet wide with a colonnaded portico six feet wide. Another substantial building measured at least sixty-one by sixty-nine feet. At some stage these buildings had been levelled to make way for an even larger structure of eighty by 110 feet. Interestingly, the floors had been laid with *tesserae* of terracotta and Presili stone, which were regarded a luxury.

One room had the added benefit of a hypocaust, with its furnace set against its outside wall. Another interesting find was a chatelaine on which keys were hung. It was thought that such a large establishment would have been an inn.

Further excavations in 1969 established that the town was lying under the modern streets of Richmond Terrace in the north, Old Oak Lane in the east and Little Water Street in the west, so that it stretched over thirty-two acres.

Further development of a commercial nature continued in the eastern part of the settlement where houses fronted a gravelled street, with some buildings incorporating both living quarters and workshops. One such building, thought to have belonged to a corn merchant, had hearths set into the walls and cobbled floors on either side of a central corridor. In the yard outside was a granary measuring fifteen by thirteen feet. This had a raised floor supported by massive timber posts to keep out the rodents. Some charred grains of wheat were also evident around the burnt out holes into which timber uprights had been inserted to support the roof, suggesting that the wheat had been accidentally burned while being roasted for malting purposes. There was also a commercial bakery close by, where a number of clay ovens were found for baking bread. Numerous stone querns were also found on the premises, which suggested that some corn grinding had taken place or perhaps had been offered as a service to the busy housewife who would normally have ground her own flour. Several Aladdin-like terracotta lamps were also recovered whole in this area. These had been filled with oil for lighting the homes.

There had also been a small industrial area located nearby, where the discovery of hearths and quantities of iron slag suggested that iron smelting had taken place. Also, an abundance of nails and iron roof fittings indicated that someone was in the trade of repairing the roofs of the timber buildings that had covered the Priory Road site. Many of the houses there had thatched roofs before the construction of stone buildings. Scraps of leather found among the rubbish in one building were a clear indication that a saddler or a cobbler had also traded there.

A thrilling discovery in the garden of 104 Priory Street was the foundations of a second-century temple. Unfortunately, its walls had been robbed in the past, so very little of the building remained. However, from this, the archaeologists were able to ascertain that the inner square – the *cella* or sanctuary – had been built within a larger square. The outside enclosure measured seventy feet square, while the inner one measured forty-four feet square. It was thought that the temple had been timber built, with panelling filled with wattle and daub, and then limewashed. This latter procedure was once a common treatment for buildings. As the temple had been built on a massive foundation pit four feet deep, it was considered substantial enough to have supported a three- or four-storey structure. The temple was small for its type, and evidence showed that it had been built before the other timber buildings around it.

31. A small selection of terracotta lamps.

The remains of some of the other surrounding buildings revealed that they had become derelict or had fallen into disuse by the second century. Others in the area had been deliberately dismantled and the site cleared. This was followed by a period of abandonment, when the site appeared to have been used for garden cultivation. But judging by the accumulation of rubbish found there, the area had eventually turned into a rubbish dump. However, even after the abandonment of this area, it appeared that people continued to lay new streets, and that occupation continued in the third century with individual trades being practised there. It was estimated that industry continued to prosper in the town for 250 years. Coins, pottery and evidence of further street maintenance suggested that life in the town of *Moridunum Demetae* continued well into the fourth century.

## The Amphitheatre

Apart from the excellent museum displaying all the possessions left behind by the soldiers and civilians housed in the old bishop's residence at Abergwili, the amphitheatre is the only Roman structure visible to visitors. It stands beside the main road leading out of Carmarthen and the bus, which also stops outside the museum, stops alongside it. Both are recommended a visit.

32. The Old Bishop's Palace at Abergwili, now the Carmarthen County Museum.

The significant discovery of the amphitheatre was made in 1936 by the acting borough engineer, who noticed a semi-circular depression in the hillside below Park Hall housing estate at the western end of Priory Street, lying just outside *Moridunum*'s boundaries. It was only because of his efforts to stop further development in the immediate area that excavations could be carried out, saving the theatre from further destruction. It had already suffered irreversible damage from the main road cutting through it and demolishing part of its seating banks.

The task of excavating the amphitheatre was carried out in 1968 by Manchester University as part of their excavation programme.

They found that the structure had probably been built in the second century by cutting into the natural hillside to form a seating bank around the arena, and was capable of seating 4,500 to 5,000 spectators, so in this respect it was smaller than the one at Caerleon.

The arena had also suffered damage by modern development, as overgrown trees and shrubs from the back gardens of the cottages lining the road had invaded its space and obscured the far end of the arena from view.

It was not known how many entrances the amphitheatre had, but several road surfaces were found, which indicated that the amphitheatre had a long period of use. Only one entrance has survived, as have the steps that led spectators up to the next row of seats.

The role of the amphitheatre appeared to have been more theatrical than gladiatorial, and would have attracted people from the surrounding areas to join in the various

33. Inside the Roman amphitheatre.

festivities and performances there. Mime plays were popular with Roman audiences, the players often wearing grotesque masks with exaggerated facial expressions to suit either their tragic or comic roles. They would have been played by men only. Musical entertainment was also very popular, so the mimed performances would be accompanied by the basic musical instruments of the day. The theatrical performances would also have religious or ritual ceremonies included. In addition to the entertainment, the army would have put on military tattoos in a display of precision and skill. Such occasions were very popular and provided great entertainment at a time when life was very basic and other social activities were rare.

In later years, further excavation of the site revealed a large grey earthenware pot containing the cremated bones of a woman. This suggested that after the amphitheatre fell into disuse, it was chosen by the people of *Moridunum* as a burial site.

Access to the site is but a few yards in from the main road, and is signposted by a large slab of slate on which the name *Moridunum* has been inscribed in large letters.

The amphitheatre is situated on the main A484 road leading out of Carmarthen, and a local bus service also operates along this route and stops immediately outside the amphitheatre. The same bus service also stops outside the Old Bishops Palace at Abergwili, the location of the County Museum.

The little habitation of Abergwili alongside the main road is also signposted along this route.

34. Bronze escutcheon, enamelled broaches and fibulae.

35. Some enamelled seal boxes with a Roman coin.

# 4

# The Gold Mines of Dolaucothi

The lure of gold brought the invading Romans to this delightful part of Demetae country, and the gold mines there were fully exploited by them. Even Tacitus, the Roman historian, was aware of their existence when he described Britain 'as being rich in gold and other ores'. The coffers in the Roman treasury were getting emptier as the Romans expanded across Europe, so the prospect of acquiring new funds inspired them to conquer this part of Celtic Wales.

The gold mines, the only ones found in Roman Wales, had been producing the precious mineral since the sixth century BC, so it was no wonder that the Romans got to know about them. Once on the scene, the Romans instantly set up a small military force across the river in nearby Pumpsaint in AD 75, the advance up from Caerleon having been very swift and decisive. Once the fortress there had been established, mining commenced immediately, with all mineral rights going to the emperor. Auxiliary troops guarded the roads along which the gold ingots travelled to their destinations at various mints, where they were turned into much-needed currency.

The mines were situated in the heart of rural Carmarthenshire in the Cothi Valley, surrounded by picturesque woodlands, so their presence was not obviously apparent. In fact, being so isolated, their existence went unnoticed for centuries after the Romans, as the latter had made no record of them. Even in the fifteenth century, when King Henry II presented the land as a gift to those families who had helped him in his struggle for the English Crown in 1545, these families were not aware that such wealth existed on their land.

The discovery of a bathhouse at the bottom of the Cothi Valley during the nineteenth century suggested that an organised settlement had been established there in the Roman era, which was verified by the finding of hundreds of pieces of domestic querns for grinding corn as well as those which had crushed the gold ore. No doubt it had been inhabited by the thousands of slaves the Romans had enlisted to mine, including convicts who served out their sentences here.

Having kept their secret for centuries, the woodlands were explored in 1844 by geologist Warington Smyth, who did a survey of the land for the then owners and discovered a cavern full of gold quartz. Eventually, the mines became part of the Dolaucothi Estate, which had been in the same Johnes family since the sixteenth century. The estate covered 2,500 acres and included several farms and the village of Pumpsaint. In the 1940s the estate was handed over to the National Trust, which has operated the mines as an ongoing tourist attraction since then, with escorted tours into the Roman levels as well as those which the Victorians mined in the nineteenth century.

The mining complex itself was surrounded by the lush woodlands of Cwm Henog, the mountain which dominated the site. The mines themselves were divided into three groups: a centrally placed cluster, a small group situated to the north and another small group in the south. While most mines go underground, the ones at Dolaucothi led inwards into the slopes of Cwm Henog, which are usually covered with bluebells every spring. The dense undergrowth has often concealed the path leading to them.

36. A quernstone.

At the bottom of Cwm Henog is a large open area that was once the opencast quarry where the Romans started their mining operations. At that time it was forty feet deeper than at present. This area is presently occupied by several buildings, with a welcoming reception in which large boards give valuable information on the production of gold throughout history. There is also a shop and a tea room. The area immediately below Cwm Henog is occupied by the corrugated buildings left by the Victorian miners who stored their equipment there. They also left behind several of the tall trolleys that once transported the gold ore around the site to the processing area.

After the Romans had exhausted the quarry they dug out two separate mines extending 160 feet into the mountain, now known as the Upper Roman Adit and the Lower Roman Adit. Both are open to visitors, but it is usually the Upper Roman Adit to which visitors are taken – its entrance almost hidden by the overgrowth of ferns. Helmets and wellington boots are provided, helmets being a necessity, and the boots useful for negotiating the woods after a rainfall.

In the Lower Adit, the most noticeable feature of the mine is its square-shaped entrance, which is typical of the way the Romans hacked their way into the rock. These square-shaped entrances can even be seen in the Roman mines on the Continent. As the ceilings of both mines rose to about seven feet, it is possible to walk upright in the Lower Roman Adit and follow the angle of the now exhausted gold seams, or even see the tool marks

37. The entrance into the Lower Roman Adit.

left behind by the miners. One such tool left behind was a gad. This had an iron head at one end of the shank and a sharp piece at the other. The sharp end was struck with a hammer so that the rock could be cut with greater precision.

Another method of extracting the ore was by building a fire against the rock face and then plunging it into cold water to cool. This process caused the ore to crack and expose the quartz, which was then removed by hand. Inside a six-foot cavern in the Lower Adit a large water tank was found sunk into the floor, as well as burnt timbers, which corroborated this simple but effective process.

A priority for the Romans was to provide ventilation for their workers. This was achieved by digging another tunnel from the Adit to the outside. In those days, light was provided by terracotta lamps fuelled by either animal fat or by oil, which gave out large amounts of offensive black and greasy smoke. When the Victorians mined there, they first had to dig a long, sloping shaft from the woodland to reach the Roman workings, and used candles they had to buy themselves. Children who worked here were forced to share the adult miners' candle light as they could not afford to buy their own.

Back in Roman times, once the ore had been extracted, it was crushed into smaller pieces by water-powered machinery consisting of suspended hammers which pounded it against a large rock lying beneath. After this operation, the broken pieces could then be crushed into even smaller pieces, either by hand-operated querns, as suggested by those found around the site, or by water-powered millstones for greater efficiency.

38. Interior walls of the Adit with number IX stamped by a miner.

After crushing, the ore was washed along a series of channels called water tables in order to separate the gold from the remaining rock waste. It was then collected at the bottom in rough material, probably a sheep's fleece as the oil in the wool helped to trap the fine grains. When the fleece was full, it was burned, leaving the gold behind. This method was favoured by the Romans, who extracted just three-quarters of a ton of gold from an estimated half a million tonnes of rock. It was found that one ton of ore had produced only a small quantity of gold, equivalent in size to a cube of sugar.

The Roman miners used the most advanced methods of technology known to them, for besides extracting the ore by hand, they also dislodged it by plying powerful jets of water on to the rock face. For this purpose, and for washing the ore afterwards, they had to build enormous reservoirs with sluices to contain the volume of water required. They also had to build aqueducts to carry it across the distance from the source of the water to the workings, often across the difficult terrain of the mountainous region. The Cothi Aqueduct alone was seven miles long and channelled 2 million gallons of water per day from a place near to source of the Cothi river. The route taken by this amazing aqueduct could be seen going along the base of the neighbouring mountain, Alt Cwm Henog, and is a testimony to the brilliance of Roman engineering. In one instance, the water had to be carried through a narrow rocky gorge and ended in a reservoir called Melin-y-Milwyr (the soldiers' mill), where, no doubt, some Roman soldiers had been recruited to join in the washing process. Today, the 'Soldiers' Mill' is nothing more than a deep depression in the woodland, with most of the water having seeped away, but it is, nevertheless, a lasting reminder of the endeavours of the Roman workmen.

The individual reservoirs at Dolaucothi were certainly among its most ingenious features. One in particular had been cut into the lower slopes of Cwm Henog and was bounded by impressive banks of up to twenty-four feet wide and forty-five feet long. A break in its banks may have allowed water to flow out to where the ore was being washed. The leat supplying this water was called Cwm Henog Leat. It also carried water to other reservoirs around the open cast. This amazing channel had been cut out of the natural rock to a depth of between three and four feet and was three feet wide. It carried water across the north-west slopes of neighbouring Alt Cwm Henog for a distance of over 1,000 feet. It was clear that parts of the channel had been reinforced with roughly built dry-stone walling and had obviously been the work of the Roman soldiers who were experts in stonemasonry. Another impressive reservoir on the lower slopes of Cwm Henog is about nine feet wide. However, the eastern end of the reservoir lies hidden beneath the dense growth of the rhododendrons, while the western end disappears into the nineteenth-century workings.

After the gold was smelted into ingots, it was transported under military escort to the coast, where it was delivered to the various mints, the main one being the Imperial Mint at Lyons. Here it was made into currency for purchasing goods such as olive oil for cooking and heating, and luxury goods such as cloth, jewellery and fine Samian ware from the factories of Gaul.

39. Neighbouring mountain of Alt Cwm Henog along which the Cothi Aqueduct travelled.

Apart from the Roman Adits, visitors are encouraged to visit those mines worked during the nineteenth and twentieth centuries, when only pickaxes were used. Marks of these can also be seen clearly along their walls.

In modern times, full-scale mining operations did not start until 1870, but in 1910 alone, 360 tonnes of gold quartz was extracted. There was also mining between 1934 and the outbreak of war in 1939, when a deep shaft was sunk down the middle of the large opencast to connect with the gold-bearing seams. Then, in 1936, a further 3,812 tonnes were mined from the old workings, but the standard techniques of separating the gold from the waste rock did not work as efficiently as before, so other methods were tried. These also failed, and in the end, as no one in Britain could treat the ore from Dolaucothi, it was sent to Hamburg in Germany for processing. This procedure came to an end when war was declared in 1939. After that, the mines were not considered practical to operate, even though there was still some gold left in the mountain, and they were consequently closed down.

In April 2000, the Cambrian Archaeological Trust invited a team of French archaeological experts to carry out a geological survey of the mines, during which they found a section of a Roman drainage wheel that had removed excess water from the Adits to prevent flooding. These wheels had a diameter of thirteen to fourteen feet and were placed in pairs along a sloping gallery so that their rotating paddles expelled the excess water. A replica of one of these wheels was made for the *Time Team* television programme, and can be seen in the former opencast mining area beneath the slopes of Cwm Henog.

Gold-bearing pyretic shale was also found on the site, its yellow-white incrustations having tiny grains of gold trapped in the dark grey- to black-coloured shale.

Although all mining had ceased after the war, the mines were considered to be of great national importance, and the underground part of Dolaucothi was leased to the Crown by the University of Wales, Cardiff, and then sublet to the National Trust during the summer months as a visitor centre. Since then, the mines have become a popular tourist attraction with thousands learning how the gold was extracted and the various techniques used.

As the mines have also been considered to be of great archaeological and scientific importance, they have been protected by the Schedule of Ancient Monuments, and as the surrounding fields are likely to contain buried archaeology, agriculture was forbidden here.

The mines are well signposted from Lampeter, and a local bus service from the main street stops outside the entrance.

# 5

# *Segontium*: Caernarvon

The Romans took another strong foothold in this part of North Wales at a place we now know as Caernarvon, which they considered to be of great strategic importance since it gave the Roman fleet control of all the shipping in the area and enabled their ships to deliver essential supplies to their troops without undue opposition from the local tribes. It also gave them control of the Menaii Straights, and strengthened their control over the conquered Lleyn Peninsular, leaving the way clear to conquer Anglesey. Across the way, they had already routed the Deceangli without mercy, as well as the Ordovices, who they had almost annihilated.

The fortress was sited at the top of Llanbeblig Hill on the outskirts of Caernarvon which, as was the Romans' preference, commanded the surrounding area. They named their fortress *Segontium*, which is thought to have been derived from the name of the local Seigont tribe who lived there, or they may have named it after the river Seigont, as they had done with naming *Isca* after the river Usk at Caerleon. Being so close to the sea and on a busy highway, the Romans had all the facilities they needed to run an efficient military post here, and it was thought that *Segontium* had also been the administrative centre for north-west Wales, to include Anglesey and encompass the tribal territories of the beleaguered Celts.

40. Lanbeblig Hill looking south, with the fortress behind railings on the right.

Early recorded evidence of the fortress's existence appeared in William Camden's fourth edition of his *Britannia* in 1594, following his visit to North Wales in 1590. In it, he made the comment that 'there is possible evidence of a Roman station near to the church of Llanbeblig'. Roman artefacts found on or near to the site had also drawn people's attention to that possibility.

In 1845, a letter addressed to the *Archaeologia Cambrensis*, which recorded all historic discoveries, stated that there was 'a subterranean passage at the bottom of the hill' and that workmen had come across what they termed a 'Roman house'. As Wales did not have museums at that time, letters also expressed concern that historic artefacts were being lost to souvenir hunters. As a result of this awareness for preserving antiquities found in Wales, museums were finally established in the country.

Confirmation of the name of *Segontium*'s garrison was provided by a broken tablet which had appeared outside the north-west guardroom, found among the rubble. It recorded the repair work of an aqueduct which had collapsed. It read:

... SEPT SEVERVS PIVS PER ... VREL ANTONINVS ... VAEDVCTIVM VETVS ... BS COH I SVNIC. RESIT.

Translated, it read:

[Under the Emperors] Septimius Severus Pius Pertinax, Marcus Aurelius Antoninus [and Publius Septimius Geta, noble Caesar]. The streams of this aqueduct, collapsed through age, were restored by the First Cohort of Sunici.

It was customary for anyone repairing any part of the fortress to record the event in this manner. The names of the emperors indicate that the aqueduct was repaired around the second century, and that the soldiers responsible for the work had been part of the *Cohors Quingenaria Equitata*, a 500-strong unit of mixed infantry and cavalry. The Sunici were a Belgic tribe living on the shores of the Rhine, and were known to have come to serve in Roman Britain around AD 124.

In 1919, members of the Cambrian Archaeological Society purchased three and a half acres of land attached to the fortress in order to stop further modern developments from taking place. As it was found that trees were also obstructing part of the site, permission had to be obtained from the vicar of Caernarvon to fell them so that the necessary excavations could be carried out. The late Sir Mortimer Wheeler, then director of the National Museum of Wales, carried out this work in the summer of 1921. And despite the close proximity of allotment gardens, two acres of the fortress were successfully excavated to reveal all the principal buildings, including two granaries, the barrack blocks and all the store houses.

At excavation, it was seen that the fortress measured 510 by 415 feet, giving an area of approximately five and a half acres, and during the work, the foundations produced a wealth of information regarding its occupation, comparable in volume to that of the fortress at Caerleon.

As with all other auxiliary fortresses, *Segontium* conformed to the same military plan – an elongated square shape with rounded corners, similar to a playing card. At first, all its defences and internal buildings were made of timber, but these were later built with stone with the addition of turrets and enormous gateways. The double roads leading into the fortress had been laid with boulders and covered over with a thick layer of local slate, and they were found to have been continually resurfaced during the fortress's long history. Two roads were found to have entered the fortress, divided by a central pier. Remarkably, their original surfaces were still intact. Inside the fortress the two principal roads were also found, one of which was the *Via Principalis*, which ran through the fortress and fronted the *Principia* – the headquarters building, which was always located in the centre of the fortress for protection purposes. This building had always been built to the highest standards, with fine architectural features to impress those arriving at the fortress. The other main road was the Via Decumana, which ran east to west and split the fortress into two halves. Just inside the defences, a pair of bronze cupids surfaced, as did another figure made of lead holding a cylindrical object which was a holder for a torch.

Surviving pottery shards and coins from the excavations of the fort's interior in 1921–23 suggested that there had been three periods of occupation: AD 75–140, 210–290, and 355 or 365, spanning well over 200 years, during which time several phases of rebuilding took place, notably in the headquarters building and the commandant's house.

Excavation of the headquarters building proved interesting. Being of great importance, it had a sculptured archway over its entrance. At the rear of the building was a range of rooms flanking the *Sacellum*, or inner sanctuary, where all the standards were kept, along with the army funds. A bust of the emperor would also have been kept there. There was also a group of five rooms for the administrative staff, and these would have been partitioned off with curtains. During the third century, a sunken safe was added inside the *Sacellum*. Being the most prestigious room in the entire fortress, it was the only room to have been lavishly decorated with coloured wall plaster. This consisted of striped patterns in bright red, yellow and green. Hidden beneath the floor was the sunken safe, five feet deep, which contained all the money. It was entered by a flight of five steps and measured ten by nine feet. Its original floor had been laid with large slabs of local stone grouted with pink cement and raised seven inches above a clay floor. It was thought that the Roman builders had intended to lay the slabs over the natural earth in order to prevent dampness during the wet weather. A thick layer of salt had also been laid to ensure complete damp-proofing. During this work, one of the builders had dropped a *denarius* of Elagabalus (AD 218–222) under one of the slabs. Three silver *denarii* were also found under some slates, one from the time of Faustina the Elder (died AD 141), one of Severus Alexander (AD 222–235) and one belonging to the reign of Julia Mamaea (died AD 235). All of these were in mint condition when lost. *Denarii* were part of a soldier's pay and, being small, they were easily lost. A surprising find in the under-floor safe was a sixteen-inch-high altar dedicated to Minerva, goddess of wisdom. It read:

DEAE MINERVAE AR SABINANVS ACT. V.S.L.M.

Translated, it read:

To the Goddess Minerva, Aurelius Sabinanus, actarius, gratefully fulfils his vow.

Minerva was also a goddess favoured by scribes, so it would appear that she had become the patron goddess of the clerical division of the army, of which Sabinanus, an *actarius*, was part. An *actarius* was a kind of quartermaster who was responsible for the securing the necessary allotment of rations to the recruits, and organised their distribution at the granaries and other storehouses. As there was no rank of quartermaster in the Roman army before the beginning of the third century, it was reasonable to assume that the altar belonged to the period before then. The style of lettering was said to have been characteristic of the third century. Another feature of the altar was that it had been made from local sandstone. The mountings showed traces of plaster or cement which had been used to conceal defects in the stone and, interestingly, traces of red paint used to highlight the letters were still visible. The altar may have ended up there because Sabinanus had hidden it there for safety, not being able to take it away with him when he left the fortress. Gangs were known to vandalise the forts after their occupants had gone, and this was something that Sabinanus did not want to happen to such a sacred item. The underground safe also revealed another interesting discovery when a fragment of an iron box was found, along with a hoard of money, which had been its contents. It was strange that this small treasure had been left behind by the withdrawing staff, implying that they had left in a great hurry. During abandonment, the trap door of the safe had been left open to allow centuries of dirt to drift into it and cover the floor to a depth of eighteen inches.

Next door to the *Principia* was the commandant's house. It was unlike any quarters found inside the fortress as, befitting his rank, he was offered a house in the style of a Mediterranean villa, complete with a courtyard with a well for his own personal water supply. The house consisted of six rooms on one side of the courtyard and four on the other. One of the rooms contained a pedestal on which a statue or an altar had stood, and is thought to have been a private shrine. The commandant's shrine had three doors giving access to the courtyard with a veranda supported by timber posts, but at a later date the timbers were replaced by a graceful colonnade. Seven of the column bases had survived in their original positions. Grand though the building was, the builders had resorted to paving the courtyard with broken roof tiles.

The granaries were lying on the opposite side of the principal buildings on either side of the *Via Principalis*, and had been divided into three storage compartments, but the line of the main Llanbeblig Road had cut through the end store on its south side. The main road had also cut across the fortress to separate the bathhouse, which lay on the opposite side of the road.

The barracks for the cohort were situated in the north-west corner of the fortress and conformed to the usual military plan by having long blocks separated by wide passageways.

Although the garrison was withdrawn in AD 290, evidence from the coins suggested that the fortress was reoccupied sixty years later. And as a result of finding so many coins at *Segontium*, archaeologists were able to date the occupation with more certainty. Coins from the reigns of Constans and Gratian (AD 367–383) were found in abundance among the uppermost floors throughout the *Principia*, including over 200 from AD 290–350, thus providing evidence that the military occupation of *Segontium* had come to an end around AD 390, soon after the reign of Carausus, when the headquarters building was finally razed to the ground.

*Above:* 41. Sunken Safe in the Sacellum at the *Segontium* Roman Fortress.

*Right:* 42. Altar found in the Sunken Safe at the *Segontium* Roman Fortress.

At this time there was a period of violence and unrest when invaders took possession of *Segontium*. It was also a time when Christians vented their disgust on the monuments and buildings they regarded as anti-Christ, either by defacing them or destroying them altogether. Taking this into account, it was not surprising that only a few inscription slabs survived. The arched entrance to the *Sacellum* also suffered the same fate, along with the stone sculptures that had appeared over the gateways. Much of the remaining stonework also disappeared when it was taken away for building purposes until, in the end, very little of the fortress remained. The only inscription to have survived was the one recording the restoration work by a cohort of the garrison in the second century. Even the tombstones from the cemetery lining the main road had been uprooted by vengeful intruders.

There was evidence that civilians in search of shelter had occupied the abandoned but disintegrating fortress, indicated by a small room occupying two-thirds of the south-eastern guard room. Unlike the well-mortared work of the Roman builders, the flimsy walls of the new structure had been roughly held together by clay. Even a few centuries later, the ruined fortress still provided some shelter for migrating families. Below the last step into the entrance a *styca* – a coin of the Northumbrian King Eaured (AD 808–840) – was found. It was a historic discovery, as it appeared to have been the earliest Saxon coin found in Wales. In fact, Northumbrian coins were rarely found outside the county. A few coins from the reign of King Edgar (AD 959–975) also surfaced.

Some surprising discoveries were made even before excavations started. In 1846, during the building of a new vicarage, workmen came across a well, five feet square and excavated to a depth of twenty-one feet. The sides of the well were composed of five-foot long oblong blocks of stone that had been chiselled and set in place without cement. Interestingly, they were found to be identical to the corner stones of Caernarvon Castle. This gave rise to the suspicion that the medieval builders had robbed the stone from the fortress. Some other surprising items also emerged from the well. These included two antlers belonging to a red deer, as well as horns from four bucks and the tusk of a small boar. There was also an accumulation of large oyster shells, nails and some pottery. Red deer and boar would have been hunted for meat – in Roman times these animals roamed the forests in large numbers. Numerous oyster shells were also found, and as they have also appeared on other sites, they were obviously a favourite among the soldiers.

A significant discovery, though, was the recovery of a complete sword near the vicarage. The blade, slightly leaf shaped, had suffered some damage through decay over the centuries and its hilt showed signs of repair. Its distinguishing feature was an ivory pommel with bronze and copper bands surrounding its base. The bands were regarded as unusual, and it is thought that the sword had belonged to a high-ranking officer at the fortress.

The original sword is in the possession of the Bangor museum, but a very good replica can be seen in the very interesting museum inside the excavated site. Another valuable discovery was a gold cross-bow brooch, two and a half inches long and four inches wide. It was dated to the fourth century, and had probably belonged to one of the civilian settlers who had made their home in the new community situated around the fortress. Another item of gold also surfaced. It was a Gnostic talisman, four inches high and only one inch wide. Its entire surface was covered with Greek symbols and lettering, the first lines of which were deciphered as being the names Adonai, Eloi, and Sabaoth. The wording also mentioned four of the seven planets, namely, the Sun, Jupiter, Mars and the Moon. The last three lines of the Greek script were deciphered as 'protect me Alphianos'. The talisman appeared to be associated with the mystic belief established in Syria during the third century, and had obviously been a 'good luck' charm to its owner. The talisman also proved interesting in that it highlighted the cosmopolitan character of the culture enjoyed by the inhabitants of *civitas Segontium* during the third and fourth centuries. Another relic was a square-shaped altar only two feet high, which had been dumped in the churchyard until someone, realising its significance, rescued it. The altar possessed an alternate design of a garland and a flagon around its four sides, although one had been defaced. The altar can also be seen at the site museum.

However, the discoveries were not yet over. In April 1985, while workmen were digging trenches to take a sewer pipe for the proposed housing site on land next to the fortress, they struck the foundations of a large structure that was to give one last glimpse into the Roman era, and particularly the religious life at *Segontium* from the first to the third century. At once, the archaeologists recognised the layout as being a *Mithraeum* – a temple dedicated to the god Mithras. The Caernarvon Council were immediately informed, and put a halt to the building work so the structure could be examined in more detail.

Excavations were carried out by the National Museum of Wales on behalf of the then Ministry of Works, and they found that the *Mithraeum* measured forty-eight by twenty-one and a half feet. Although much of the foundations had been destroyed long before the modern-day workmen struck them, much of its architectural plan was still recognisable. Evidence showed that the temple had lived through a period of great activity at the fortress, and that the life of the temple continued into the third century in conjunction with the large civilian settlement that had established itself on all three sides around the fortress. It also appeared that the temple had been built in three phases. As excavations progressed, many aspects of the temple emerged, including an antechamber with an alcove. This was a shrine where images of Mithras were displayed. The room measured thirty-five by eighteen feet. As one of the essential elements of a *Mithraeum* was a windowless sunken nave to represent the cave in which Mithras killed the bull, the nave would have been lit by candles. The earlier finding of the cupid torch bearer was thought to have been part of the lighting arrangements. No less than twelve candle holders were found in the northern end of the building, where they had illuminated the sanctuary area containing the shrine. At least six of the candle holders had come from the same mould.

The nave was thirty-five feet long and had a raised floor covered with gravel. Down either side of the nave were wooden benches on which the participants sat. These had probably been covered with hides or fur for extra comfort.

In the south wall of the nave was an entrance five feet wide and finished with a sill of soft pink sandstone, but the step leading down into the antechamber had been destroyed by the work for the housing estate. Outside the antechamber there was a patch of cobbling, which suggested that some kind of shelter had been erected over it.

The temple had been roofed with purple Cambrian slate, which had been obtained locally. These individual slabs were thought to have weighed between nine and fourteen pounds each and measured sixteen by fourteen and a half inches thick. Cambrian slate was also exported to Chester. This roof, built in Phase 1 of the construction, was rendered safe by the

43. An aerial view of Caernarvon. The *Segontium* Roman Fortress is visible to the extreme right of the picture; it is the beige patch in the middle of the built-up area.

insertion of timber colonnades inside the temple during Phase III. Ten bases were found, each one having a central, squared mortise to fit the base of the post. Only a few of the bases had remained in their original places. The others had probably been used as altar pedestals.

In the foundations were two shards of first- and second-century pottery, including a flagon and three denarii of Faustina. A complete beaker and tin cup that had presumably been used in the ceremonies were also found, as was a chain made from fine links. Beneath the altar lay fragments of ironwork, including a tiny bell only one inch high. Even its clapper had survived. Several of these fragments were then placed together to form a two-branched candle holder which is considered to be of an unusual type. The socket at the base suggested that the candelabrum had been fixed to a pole and carried as a standard during the ceremonies, and that the little bell, with others, had been suspended from it by the chain to make a ringing noise as the standard was carried down the nave.

When the rubble in the nave was cleared, the brown soil changed into a layer of ash and charcoal in which were fragments of large, squared oak beams. Below this was a thin film of brown earth directly on top of the Phase III floor. There was little doubt that this represented a period of abandonment when the temple had lost its roof and had been opened to the elements.

No cult sculptures were found anywhere in the temple apart from its altars. This suggested that they had been destroyed by vengeful intruders.

Only six Mithraic temples have been found in Britain so far. The others were located at Walbrook in south-east England, three on Hadrian's Wall, and the last one emerged in the City of London, not far from St Paul's Cathedral. And while Mithraic sculptures were found at Caerleon, Carmarthen, Chester, Carlisle and Castlesteads, suggesting that *Mithraeum* were there, none of their buildings could be found.

Like the fortress beside it, *Segontium*'s *Mithraeum* had fallen into irreversible decline and had its walls robbed, almost down to the foundations. But through the good fortune of modern excavation, its resurrection has given a good account of its past history.

# 6
## *Viroconium*: Wroxeter

The Romans chose to site another military fortress here, close to the eastern borders of Wales, just north of their other small fortresses in the Leintwardine area.

This was the territory ruled by the Cornovii tribe, and the fortress was necessary to guard an important river crossing which would have been crucial for ferrying goods and supplies along its stretches, as well as for commanding the Severn Valley, which offered easy access into central Wales. The Romans called it *Viroconium*, meaning 'the Town of Virico of the Cornovii', referring to Virico, the chieftain who had suffered the same fate as his warriors when the soldiers of the Fourteenth Legion burnt down their strongholds on the Wrekin to the north-west. In modern geographical terms, Wroxeter is now situated in the English county of Shropshire.

The fortress itself was just large enough to sustain a small military force to control movement in the area, and measured only 515 feet east to west, and 470 feet north to south. It was defended with two large V-shaped ditches on its northern side, one being fourteen feet wide and eight feet deep, and the other ten feet wide and six feet deep. Although all the ditches had become silted up, they produced fragments of good quality Samian ware, which the soldiers had dumped there. There was no sign of any internal stone buildings, so it is thought that the fortress had been built entirely of timber, which had rotted away over the centuries. However, in 1783, the discovery of a tombstone with a Latin inscription and a relief showing a mounted horseman striking down an escaping enemy was crucial in identifying the fortress as having been occupied by the Thracian Cohort, which was a part mounted unit who had come from the region of modern Bulgaria. The relief clearly indicated the chief role of these troopers after a battle, when they had to strike down the enemy escaping from the battlefield. Other stone carvings have portrayed these troopers riding bareback as it gave them greater freedom to lean more forward in the saddle to perform their gruesome task. The tombstone read:

TIB CLAVD TIRINTIVS EQ COH THRACVM ... ANNORVM LVII STIPENDIOR XX ... HSE.

Which translated means:

Tiberius Claudius Tirintius, Trooper of the Thracian Cohort ... aged fifty-seven years with twenty-... years' service ... he lies here.

This historic stone now resides in the museum of Rowleys House at Shrewsbury.

Another significant discovery was a bronze Diploma, or military discharge, which was awarded to auxiliary soldiers on completion of twenty-five years' service, and granted Roman citizenship to both them and their families. The Diplomas also legalised any marriages they made while on service. It was also possible for the recipient to receive a copy of the Diploma

*Above:* 44. A view of *Viroconium* (Roman Wroxeter) from the air.

*Right:* 45. A close-up view of the ruined site from the air.

with the addition of his name and unit. One such Diploma was found at Wroxeter bearing the name of Mansuetus, an ex-infantryman of the Second Cohort of Dalmatians and dated to AD 130. In all, three Diplomas were found inside Cornovian territory, which suggested that all the soldiers had chosen to retire from military service in this part of Roman Wales.

Many soldiers of the Fourteenth Legion, known as Legio Gemina XIV, another of the big four legions invading Britain, were also buried here after a period of retirement. One, whose name was Titus Flaminius, had come from Northern Italy and had served with the legion for twenty-two years before dying at the age of forty-five. His tombstone recorded that he had been an *aquilifer*, someone who carried the legion's eagle standard. This was a tall staff surmounted by an eagle, and he would have worn the ceremonial headdress made from a wolf's head. The role of an *aquilifer* was considered to have been a great honour. Another tombstone recorded the name of Marcus Petronius who was said to have been a *signifer*, also a standard bearer. A soldier of the Twentieth Legion, known as Legio XX Valeria Victrix, which passed through here on its way up from Devon to establish its own legionary fortress at Chester, was also buried here. He was named as Gaius Mannius Secundus, son of Gais, from a tribe in Northern Italy. He was fifty-two years of age when he died after serving thirty-one years of military service.

After the fortress had ceased to function during the second half of the first century, it was demolished and the site cleared to make way for the new settlement, which the people of the Cornovii had started to build after being ousted from their strongholds.

Excavations in 1913 revealed that the town probably started as a timber-built settlement around AD 80, and that the pioneer settlers had built a defensive wall six feet thick around the town as a safeguard, which had been made up of large cobbles obtained from a nearby quarry. The cobbles had been built on a layer of clay without mortar, and as an extra defence, the settlers also laid a berm – an area between the ditches and the parapet – eleven feet wide. They also created deep ditches with a forty-five degree slope, similar to those of any fortress.

By the middle of the second century the town of *Viroconium* had grown into a site of an estimated 200 acres and had become a prestigious market town whose citizens enjoyed an era of peace and reconciliation, and reaped the benefits of the Roman way of life which had been offered to them.

By the fourth century, *Viroconium* had grown to be the fourth-largest town in Roman Wales, and became the provincial capital of *Britannia Secunda*, the name given to Roman Wales. It also became the administrative and tribal capital of the Cornovii – similar to when the citizens of Caerwent were granted full autonomy. *Viroconium* then became *Viroconum Cornovorium*. This title was regarded as unique, not only within the province of Roman Britain but across the Roman Empire itself.

A ceremonial plaque with a Latin inscription was found in the ruins of the forum and provided valuable information as to the identity of the town. It reads:

IMP CAES DIVI TRAIANI PARTHICI FIL DIVI NERVAE NEPOTI
TRAIANO HADRIANO AVG PONTIFICI MAXIMO TRIB POT XIIII COS
III PP CIVITAS CORNOVIORVM

This translates as:

To emperor Ceasar Trajanus Hadrianus Augustus, son of the divine Trajanus Parthicus, the grandson of the divine Nerva, chief priest holding tribunician power for the fourteenth time, Consul three times, father of the country, the city of the Cornovii erected this.

This plaque had probably been given pride of place over the entrance of the forum, and with the naming of the tribal council, it has the same historical status as the inscription at Caerwent.

The only Roman building to have survived on the site is the great wall of the basilica, which was built on to the baths. It was an enormous structure, 245 feet long and sixty-seven feet wide, and was used as an exercise hall. The great wall, called 'The Old Work' since the sixteenth century, was seventy-two feet long, and made of red sandstone blocks. It stood twenty feet above the ground, making it the tallest Roman structure to be still standing in Britain. Today, it certainly makes an impressive entrance into the excavated bathing complex.

In Roman times, the basilica had been divided by colonnades just like the one at *Venta*, with a central nave thirty feet wide and two aisles each estimated to have been fourteen feet wide. The basilica would have had an enormous roof, which was estimated to have been sixty feet high. It was also revealed, from fragments found, that the walls of the basilica had been plastered with coloured stucco and its floors covered with fine mosaics. A piece of walling revealed an attractive circular design in royal blue against a white background. The floor of the central nave had a herring-bone pattern of red brick, while the aisles had mosaic floors with plain geometric designs in panels of about eight and a half by eighteen feet, coloured in a greenish-black with traces of red on creamy white. Another mosaic, measuring fifteen feet square, also had a geometric design, but in red, green, grey and purple colours. This one has unfortunately been destroyed, but someone had the foresight of making a drawing of it for posterity. In the debris were several padlocks, a chain link, a trident candlestick and, curiously, a steel axe. Fragments of sculptured stone also suggested that the building had been well decorated with stunning architectural features such as statuary and Corinthian columns.

Once through the basilica wall with its enormous square opening, the extensive bathing complex is immediately visible and stretches to the far end of the site, comparable in size to a football pitch. All the brick pillars of the hypocausts are still in their original positions, and a great many of them are standing at least three to four feet high. For the benefit of the modern-day visitor, the different sections of the baths have been gravelled in different colours.

In Roman times, bathers entered the *frigidarium* from the basilica through double doors now marked in black gravel. Leading off this room on either side was the *tepidarium*, and to the side of this were the dry heat rooms (*laconia*), where bathers were allowed to sweat. Beyond this was the *caldarium*, the hot bathing room. The floors of the latter two were lower than those of the *frigidarium* as this allowed the heat to circulate more efficiently from the furnace at the far end. Then, for reasons of economy, these two rooms were closed down in the third century, turning the old *laconia* into a new *tepidarium*, and creating a new *caldarium* with a furnace. The baths with all their assets were a great social outlet and, according to a contemporary letter, had become noisy from boisterous bathers.

The letter, written by a woman who had rooms above the baths, complained about the constant noise coming from them. She complained about those who suddenly burst into song, and especially the cries of the food and drink sellers, the pie man and those from the restaurants who touted for business, all of whom were making her life intolerable with their melodic calls. The letter was a great historical find, and portrayed a vivid picture of the daily occurrences at the baths. One can almost see the bathers splashing about in the water – their voices reverberating around the great rooms as they called out to one another and all mingling with the cries of the different sellers. Remnants of small animal bones such as chicken and oyster shells were a clear indication that the bathers enjoyed snacking in between their baths.

The south-west corner of the baths was where the *macellum* or market had been, and was entered through a portico. This had later been altered to include sets of square rooms with a surrounding courtyard for selling high-quality goods and food. There was also a forum. It occupied a large area and had a piazza in its centre, which doubled as a market place, as at Caerwent. The excavated foundations of these shops and the courtyard have been left exposed so it is possible to walk among them. The deep drainage system devised by the Romans is also visible. The basilica and its forum apparently went out of use during the fourth century.

Just south of the forum and facing Watling Street were the remains of yet another great building measuring ninety-eight feet overall, which had been built during the second century. The remains of sculptured stonework and statuettes identified it as a temple. The discovery of two altars showed that the temple had been dedicated to Jupiter. Its façade was fronted by six columns nearly two feet in diameter and it was about fifteen feet high. The temple also had a cobbled courtyard surrounded by a wall two feet thick. In the eastern side of the courtyard was a line of stone foundations which appeared to have supported a series of wooden porticoes with wooden roofs covering a walkway. The bones of an ox, which had probably been slaughtered as a sacrifice, were found in the south-eastern corner. The temple was said to have been similar to the Temples of Apollo and Isis at Pompeii.

It is suspected that there is another temple lying to the north of the forum with another one to the south-east of the bathing complex. The foundations of this latter temple measured approximately 100 by fifty feet, and since it occupied a prime position in the centre of the town it must have been considered extra special. Coins of Philip I, Trajan II, Decius and Gallienus helped to date it to the third century.

*Viroconium* had a well-laid-out street system dividing it into rectangular blocks for residential homes, some of which had contained as many as twenty rooms. This marked it as another town that had prospered well. The homes had been equipped with baths and flushing toilets, and to accommodate such a demand on the water supply, which also served the civic baths, the waters of the River Severn's tributary were diverted along a V-shaped viaduct to enter the town through its eastern defences.

Among the rubble of the excavations, remnants of slag were found that had come from bronze smelting, from which bronze objects such as fibulae and brooches had been made. One of the brooches was in the form of a cockerel, and a bronze head of a woman was thought to have come from a mould made out of wax. There was also a set of tiny toilet implements hanging on a single ring. Apart from metalworking, the townspeople had also been involved with glass blowing and leather tanning.

The excavations also exposed the gravel floors of the former military barracks beneath the basilica and the baths in 1969, in which were found three lead-weighted darts or javelin heads. Curious finds were also made in the cemeteries lying to the east and north of the town. In 1810 several earthen urns and a glass vessel fourteen inches in diameter with two handles were found; they contained small cremated bones and silver coins. The graves also revealed several lamps, silver buckles and a small bronze mirror. Another bronze object thought to have been a lancet with a short blade was found inside a wooden box lined with leather. A bodkin was also found in its own little box with its copper lock amazingly still intact.

During the fifth century, the town suffered a catastrophic fire, which caused the aforementioned ceremonial plaque to fall from its place of honour, and stacks of *mortaria* and Samian bowls were found among the ruins, suggesting they might have been the entire stock of one of the shops there before it collapsed.

There were abundant traces of burning throughout the excavations, and a gruesome discovery of several sets of human remains was made inside one of the hypocausts, suggesting that the small group had hidden there to escape the fire, but had become trapped in such a confined space while the fires raged and had suffocated from the intense smoke. The skeletal remains included three women, an old man and a child. Three of the group had died in a crouching position while the other two had been lying down. Curiously, near to the old man's body was a pile of coins. A number of nails and decomposed wood adhering to the coins implied that the coins had been contained in a wooden box and that the old man had taken it with his day's takings into the hiding place. There were 132 coins in total. They ranged from the reigns of Tetricus to Constantine II to Valens, the latest coin indicating that the town had burnt down during the fifth century.

The surviving column bases of the colonnade that had fronted the forum provided a suitable boundary at the edge of the Roman excavations, as beyond the bases lay the unexplored forum and the rest of *Viroconium* lying beneath the adjoining fields. Only when the turf is removed can the rest of the town be explored.

In time, a new town emerged from the ruins of *Viroconium* to become the modern-day Wroxeter.

For non-motorists, the site is accessible by bus from Shrewsbury's bus station, which will stop close to the entrance.

46. A gritty *mortaria* with pouring lip for pulverising food.

# 7

# *Mediolanum*: Whitchurch

Having moved northwards from Wroxeter, the Roman army reached the territory occupied by the Ordovican people on the eastern borders of Roman Wales, at a place we now know as Whitchurch in the county of Shropshire, and established a fortress there. The Romans called it *Mediolanum* after the Celtic word *medio* meaning 'in the middle of', which it was, located between Wroxeter and Chester.

The fortress was identified by its western defences lying alongside the modern town's high street, and black-burnished and red buff pottery made in the Severn Valley and found in the demolished ditches dated the demolition of the fortress to around AD 100. The site then became available for the native inhabitants to enlarge their community.

Excavations beginning in 1956 in the Yardington area of the modern town soon found timber buildings and clay floors of dwellings that were typical of those built in the first century. The dwellings also contained patches of charcoal, where furnaces for metalworking had stood. The signs were that these homes had occupied that site long before the fortress was built. The early settlers also built their homes southwards along Watling Street, and as there were several furnaces found in the area, it suggested that the settlers had become self sufficient and industrious throughout the second century. Quantities of lead chippings were also found to confirm that kilns for lead smelting had taken place there, and bronze also.

As they lived in dangerous times, the townspeople thought it prudent to defend their homes with a clay rampart twenty-seven feet wide, which they built with an outer ditch around their town. These defences followed the line of the hill, and using the techniques of their past masters, they made use of the natural clay for the rampart. A stone wall in front of the rampart was added around AD 170. A portion of *Mediolanum*'s second-century rampart was found in the Yardington-Bargates area of the modern town, and had survived to a few feet high.

The residents of this early settlement found that the area of Dodington provided them with a suitable burial place, and here again it was evident that families had placed the cremated remains of their loved ones in a variety of containers, the most popular being flagons and storage jars. Someone had even removed the handles of one flagon for use as a cinerary urn. Many of the containers had been decorated with simple designs. Some examples of these first- and early second-century specimens are now on display at the Whitchurch Museum.

In the middle of the second century, many of the timber buildings were used for industrial purposes, as indicated by the quantities of charcoal and furnace rakings found on rough mortared floors. A post hole suggested that one of the workshops had been covered with an open sided shed. This industrial activity was carried out on the immediate fringe of the high street, but by the end of the century, when expansion put a premium on available land, this industry was forced away from the centre. It may have moved to the Yardington area, where evidence of continued metalworking was found. This industry was seen to continue well into the third century, when the settlement of *Mediolanum* reached its peak to emerge as a well-established town in its own right.

As *Mediolanum* grew in statue, its citizens began to have greater expectations for their town and they pulled down the timber buildings to replace them with more robust stone ones. The clay and cobbled foundations of one such structure was found lying almost up against the old defences. The building was described as 'a courtyard type' and possessed a portico with its colonnade enclosing a central courtyard. The columns had been supported by a wide base two feet high, and the design also included a walkway paved with pebbles set in clay. It would appear that while the design of the house had advanced, some of the basic methods of building were still being applied. But only the cobbled foundations of this splendid house survived, along with one course of its walling. Both its internal and external walls, which had been three feet thick, had been strong enough to support an upper storey. The foundations revealed the entire layout of the house, which had included eight rooms. The largest, thought to have been the living room, measured eighteen feet across, but the portico's columns added another eight feet to its width, making the total measurement, including the portico, twenty-six feet. A grand room indeed! Outside the house was a section of a U-shaped drain containing pieces of roofing slate thought to have been brought from Flintshire. Remarkably, nails attached to the timbers were still in place. A large area of the earth-beaten floor had also survived, but it was found that the building had been partially robbed of its stone. Comparative buildings were found at Caerwent.

There was evidence that light industry had also taken place over the site of this building when a mortared floor, up to seven inches thick, was discovered and, judging from the grooves in the mortar, a windbreak had been installed. Inside the furnace bowl was a mixture of charcoal and clinker, which had come from the collapsed dome of the furnace during the last firing and contained pieces of lead that had been cut into larger sheets. At the other end of the site, a trough kiln over eleven feet long was found cut into the footings of the south wall of Room 4 and was entirely filled with charcoal. This particular kiln had been used for evaporating brine obtained from the neighbouring springs – the same springs that had made Whitchurch a salt-producing centre in the medieval period. The method of producing salt was to keep the brine simmering in shallow vessels over a charcoal fire to produce crystals, when the salt would be scooped off. A circular pit for crystallisation was found nearby, and this was probably where the salt had been scooped off. Another interesting discovery was a small furnace. This had been cut into the clay and cobbled foundations of Room 2 and contained quantities of iron slag.

It was also apparent that another stone building had been built over the previous building and had possessed a hard-packed earth and gravel surface into which a coin of Tacitus (AD 275–76) had been trodden, giving the approximate date for the building as towards the end of the third century. A length of walling had also survived, and like its neighbour it also had a long lifespan. Prior to re-cutting the drain for this building, broken crockery and other rubbish had been used to level up the ground. In the rubble was a black burnished pie dish. This dated the occupation of the house to well into the fourth century. The rubbish also contained waste from another furnace, with remnants of some finely decorated Samian ware that had been discarded by the occupiers.

Adjoining the building was a length of walling at least fifty-eight feet long, which belonged to another stone structure with an internal wall enclosing a room that had been re-floored and raised by six inches. Fragments of coloured wall plaster showed that its decoration had been a little more upbeat than its neighbour, having had its wall patterned in red, green and white. Several fragments of glass were recovered, ranging from the thicker green-blue glass of the early second century to the thinner white window glass thought to have belonged to the fourth century, suggesting that this house had also survived a long occupation. An interesting discovery in the cobbling of what was thought to have been the entrance to the house was a series of holes created by the insertion of roughly cut timbers of not more than four inches square and trimmed into a triangle shape. This particular structure could not have carried much weight, so it might have been a hitching rail for tethering horses.

A bizarre discovery beneath the floor of one room was an under-floor grave containing the skeletal remains of a young adult male of about twenty to thirty years of age. The skeleton had a circular hole in the skull just above the right ear. The hole indicated that the young man had undergone surgery to the head known as trepanation, when a circular piece of bone is removed from the skull. Curiously, this circular piece of bone had been replaced before burial. This burial suggested that something quite sinister had occurred in that room. Firstly, it was against Roman law to bury adult corpses within a settlement, and if the young man had died on the operating table, then the surgical team, perhaps in trying to conceal a botched-up job, had committed another crime in concealing his death and hiding his body under the floor. Obviously, this crime was never discovered, so the culprits, whoever they were, had escaped Roman justice and had taken their deadly secret to their graves.

Examination of the young man's skeleton also revealed that he had been five feet tall with a good physique, but that his wisdom tooth had badly decayed, which would have caused him considerable pain, and this was probably the reason why he had sought medical help. Examination of the hole showed that it had been cut with a circular saw, similar to the kind used in today's operations. The saw also had a projecting spike attached to it.

This kind of operation had been carried out for centuries, but in the Middle Ages it was used rather barbarically on people with mental illnesses, assuming that cutting a hole in their heads would release the 'evil spirits' thought to be there and cause the pain to escape. Taking into consideration that these operations were conducted without an anaesthetic, it was no wonder that people died during the procedure. However, the operation conducted on this young man was the first evidence of trepanation having been carried out in Roman Britain. Another discovery in that grave was that one of the culprits had dropped the lid of a castor box beside the body. This dated the burial to the fourth century. Castor, commonly used in medicine, had perhaps been administered to the young man for some reason during that fateful operation.

Quantities of animal bones in some areas of the town suggested that cattle had been slaughtered in large numbers for consumption. Idyllic pastures existed for grazing, and with the production of salt for curing, the meat could be transported for marketing. Its exportation would have certainly been a contributing factor in presenting *Mediolanum* as a market town when agriculture had taken the place of light industry. And as the production of salt continued long after the thirteenth century, *Mediolanum* emerged to become the thriving market town we know today.

# 8

# *Deva*: Chester

It was here, in the extreme north-eastern corner of Wales, that the Twentieth Roman Legion stamped their authority in AD 78 with the establishment of a legionary fortress on the eastern banks of the River Dee. It was a strategic decision to site it here as it could control the Dee's estuary and, like Caernarvon, it enabled their fleet to deliver supplies and men right to its door. The location of the fortress also enabled the Roman Governor, Agricola, to launch his offensive across Deceangli lands and invade Anglesey, where he annihilated the druids.

The legion was also firmly placed to control the Deceangli lands, where there were lucrative lead mines in what is now Flintshire. A length of lead water piping had Vespasian's name clearly upon it, putting the construction date of the fortress around the end of the first century and during the final phases of the conquest of Wales. It is known that the lead mines were operational before the Romans arrived and were probably another incentive to occupy this part of Roman Wales. The mines were also fully exploited by the Romans, with great quantities of lead being transported to the fortress.

The other purpose of the legion was to impose a barrier between North Wales and the Pennines in order to prevent the tribes in those areas from coming south to support the Deceangli. But with the fall of Anglesey, the conquest of North Wales was complete.

The first task of the legion was to build a quay beside the west gate to allow ships bringing in supplies to anchor there. But as the river also ran along the southern defences, it provided a natural defence.

The legion gave their new fortress the Celtic name of *Deva*, after the river, meaning 'goddess', arising from the fact that both the Romans and Celts considered that all rivers had divine spirits. The name *Deva* appeared many times among the 125 routes mentioned in the *Antonine Itinerary*, first as Iter II (Route 2) from Hadrian's Wall to the port of *Rutupiae* (Richborough) in Kent, which had been the port where the Roman legions had landed from the Continent. On this route, *Deva* was mentioned as Deva Leg XX Vict after the legion. It also featured on Iter XI as the route from *Segontium*. Its subsequent name, *Deva Victrix*, appeared on the *Ravenna Cosmography* of the seventh century. The title Victrix was an honour bestowed by the emperor on those legions who had helped in the defeat of Boudicca's rebellion. The fact that the legion was placed here also had a military significance: it lay on Watling Street, which was one of the great arterial roads of Roman Britain, running from London to Wroxeter where it met the Roman road going from Chester to its sister legionary fortress at York. There was no doubt that the success of the Roman advance throughout Wales had resulted from the construction of this vast network of roads, which also connected all the fortresses. This meant that the soldiers were only one day's march away from each other in case reinforcements were required to deal with sudden attacks and other emergencies.

On the evidence of eleven tombstones found on the site, the construction of this great legionary fortress, which had been manned by a full complement of 6,000 men, had been assigned to the soldiers of the Second Legion Adiutrix Pia Fidelis, shortened to Legio

II Adiutrix, but they were eventually withdrawn from Britain in AD 86. Men of the Twentieth Legion, known as Legio XX Valeria Victrix, thereafter became the permanent garrison. They would give the name of Deva Victrix to the fortress.

When the men of the Twentieth Legion arrived, the fortress was only ten acres in extent, but they enlarged it to a massive 59.8 acres, making it larger than Caerleon. The fortress then measured 1,930 feet north to south, and 1,340 feet across. The extra space was to provide accommodation for the governor, his staff and bodyguard of 1,000 men. This required a massive workforce capable of building large structures, at which the Roman army was expert, and for which massive quantities of wood, perhaps from a woodland nearby, was required to build its internal buildings and defences. But, according to army practice, the timber buildings were replaced with stone after the commencement of the second century. Again, the Roman builders used local materials such as sandstone blocks obtained from quarries lying just across the river.

Such a powerful fortress had to be defended. It was surrounded by a sandstone wall twenty-two feet high and had rectangular towers, twenty-one and a half to twenty-two feet wide, built at each corner, including twenty-six along the sides and spaced at approximate intervals of 200 feet. They projected seventeen feet back from the rear face of the fortress wall, and had been solidly built with no interiors, suggesting that they had served as platforms for the heavy catapult machines or *ballistae* that the Romans used for hurling stone balls at the enemy. A large number of these balls were recovered in various places around the excavations. Six of the stone towers were successfully excavated and the remains of the south-east corner tower can be seen at close quarters from the roadside. Internal turrets completed the defences.

Behind the ramparts and along the *intervallum* – the road which encircled the fortress – was a line of narrow buildings, also built with sandstone. They were about seventy feet long. Close by were circular ovens, which were thought to have been the cookhouses. Fortunately a large section of the northern wall had survived to a height of sixteen feet, and can also be viewed from the bridge over the canal, which was once a defensive ditch. This stretch of the fortress wall is one of the permanent reminders of the Roman occupation, and is the only Roman wall in Europe to have survived in such a good state of preservation.

During 1883 and 1892, about ninety inscribed tombstones were found built into a section of the wall. The enclosed location certainly helped to preserve these unique memorials. One such memorial stone had the name of Gaius Lovesius Cadarus, a soldier of the Twentieth Legion. Another tombstone was dedicated to Gabininius Felix, a soldier of the Second Augusta Antoniniana Legion, which was garrisoned at Caerleon. He had probably died while visiting comrades at *Deva*. The best of these unique memorials are now on display at the city's Grosvenor Museum. An altar also surfaced. It bore the following Latin inscription:

GENIO SANCTO CENTVRIE AELIVS CLAVDIAN OPT. VS

Which translated to:

Aelius Claudianus, optio, fulfils his vow to the sacred Genius of his century.

An *optio* was a junior officer next in command to a centurion. He was responsible for book keeping. A *genius* was a 'guardian spirit' – a statuette of one was found in Caerleon. On the side of the altar was a relief of an axe and a knife, with a jug and a saucepan on the other side. All of these items would have been used in the religious ceremonies held at the altar. Sometimes, an altar would be used as a marker for a grave, as in this instance.

The Romans believed that the soul lived on after death, and many of the gravestones at the museum reflect this belief. One in particular depicted the deceased, Cynthia Dinysia, reclining on a couch and drinking from a wine glass, presumably celebrating her life in paradise. Below the sculpture, an inscription told us that she was forty years of age and that it had been erected by her heirs. Another showed a bearded man, likewise celebrating with a glass of wine. The tombstones also had images of birds and various fruits incorporated into their designs. They are the largest collection of Roman tombstones in Britain, and are fun to see.

As the modern city was built over the entire fortress, including the civilian settlements located around it, not much of Roman *Deva* survived, but the excavations did reveal many interesting buildings that had once formed the great city. They have given us an interesting picture as to how it must have looked.

It all started in 1725 when the demolition of the Feathers Inn unearthed the foundations of a vast rectangular building, 250 feet long and eighty feet wide. This was identified as the basilica to the fortress baths, which had been built close to the south gate. This structure, which also functioned as a huge exercise hall, was thirty-four feet wide, and had two rows of columns creating an aisle eighteen feet wide on either side, similar to those in Caerwent and Wroxeter. The basilica also contained an adequately sized swimming pool. An interesting discovery was a decorative mosaic with a pattern in red, white and blue. Unfortunately the excavations of 1863 considerably damaged the mosaic beyond repair, so very little of it survived. It was only though the foresight of a member of the Chester Archaeological Society that photographs were taken and a written record was made, so the valuable details of the mosaic were not entirely lost. A small piece of stone broken from a Latin inscription was found in the basilica and firmly dated the baths to the reign of Vespasian, at the time when the fortress was being built at the end of the first century.

Excavations to the east of the basilica were made between 1909 and 1910, and again in 1926–27. These exposed the massive columns supporting the basilica's enormous roof. Another beautiful mosaic was also found in the *frigidarium* featuring sea creatures. Large-scale excavations were then conducted under modern Pepper Street in 1964, during which the three main bathing areas were located with their hypocausts still intact. But again, these valuable remains were tragically destroyed when building work commenced on the Grosvenor shopping centre in 1963–64. The inadequate archaeological examination of the baths was blamed on the lack of resources, but the 'marine' mosaic did survive and the plan of the complex was recorded for posterity.

However, the excavation of the baths emphasised many of the delightful aspects of Roman architecture, with examples of exemplary workmanship, and again no expense appeared to have been spared by the military in providing luxurious facilities for their soldiers. In the *caldarium*, there were semi-circular recesses containing communal wash basins, as well as large bathing pools. The pool at the west end of the *caldarium* was

47. Tombstone of a
forty-year-old woman now in
the Grosvenor Museum.

about thirty-three feet across and lay in an apsidal bay, which projected from the main body of the building so as to receive the maximum amount of sunlight. Several furnaces were found in the south-east of the complex. These supplied heat to the *caldarium*'s pool and wash basins. There were also two large cold-water reservoirs that fed an open-air swimming pool. The main water reservoir had rested on a concrete base, thirty-five feet long and three feet thick, which was supported on fifteen sandstone blocks arranged in three rows of five. The amount of water required to feed the individual baths, wash basins, fountains and swimming pools was extensive, and was estimated to be in the region of 850,000 litres per day. To maintain such a massively sophisticated and intensely used complex was a major undertaking. This is especially apparent when taking into consideration the fact that the maintenance could not be undertaken until the last bather had left, when each pool would have had to be drained and cleaned before the first bathers arrived in the morning, especially if the water had been polluted by oil from the bathers' bodies. Also, by morning there would have to be an adequate amount of hot water to feed the wash basins. This could only be achieved by ensuring that there was plenty of wood available to feed the nine furnaces. This enterprise alone was said to have required several tons of wood to supply the minimum of 63,000 litres of hot water each morning. It was also estimated that the amount of cold water required to fill the swimming pools, fountains and the cold baths was in the region of 55,000 litres per day. Since water was an essential requirement for flushing the latrines, drinking and cooking, another 15,000 litres was added to each day's requirements. The source for this enormous amount of water was Broughton, a mile to the east. Water was channelled along an aqueduct to the fortress. Lead piping carried this water to its various destinations, and was found in three places along the aqueduct's route. Waste water was generally routed along stone-covered drains to discharge into the main channel running underground on the side of the roads. It is interesting to note that all the fortress baths were the forerunners of the great imperial baths in Rome from the first century onwards.

As the general maintenance of the baths show, the garrison appeared to have been working around the clock. Apart from being an efficient fighting force they were also responsible for all maintenance work and looking after the condition of the roads, repairing them whenever necessary, thus keeping their workshops and saw mills active throughout the day and night. The baths remained in use until the fourth century, but while their remains have mostly been destroyed, the hypocaust of the *sudatorium* (the steam room) survived and is left exposed for public viewing in the cellar of commercial premises in Bridge Street. The hypocaust is well lit and can be reached down a flight of steps. It is interesting to note the height of the pillars and the amount of space they occupied under the floor.

During the excavations in the 1960s, quantities of animal bones and charcoal from fires were found inside the baths, which suggested that after the Romans had abandoned them, civilians occupied them over as living quarters, just like they had done at Caerleon.

Five massive column bases were found lying in the cellar of No. 23 Northgate Street. They were identified as being part of the north colonnade of the judgement hall which had lain behind the basilica's courtyard, and several years later, in nearby Goss Street, the colonnaded west front was found. They were estimated to have been 122 feet long and 244 feet to 250 feet wide. Other extraordinary structures located within the fortress were two enormous buildings, which may have accounted for the need for the extra space. The first, measuring 480 feet long and 180 feet wide, had a courtyard, an inner colonnaded portico and an outer range of rooms. Its unusual ground plan featured a long rectangular structure in its centre. This had been built in stone, but strangely, work had apparently stopped then restarted again after a lapse of some ten years, when its layout was changed to add smaller rooms with wider doors. The purpose of the building has not been determined and remains a mystery.

The second additional building measured 180 by 100 feet overall and was described as elliptical as it possessed an oval inner courtyard. This structure was also surrounded by a colonnaded portico, behind which was an encircling range of twelve wedge-shaped rooms all with enormous arched doorways, twelve feet wide. In the centre of the courtyard was the foundation for a sculptured fountain. It was here that the length of water piping running up to its base was found, on which the names of Vespasian and his son Titus were stamped. This immediately dated the piping to AD 79. It was also the only example of Roman lead piping to have been found in Britain and is on display at the Grosvenor Museum.

Adjoining the courtyard of the second building was a large bathing complex occupying more than half of the width of the building. These baths were said to have required an estimated 80,000 litres of water per day. Despite the presence of the baths, there was no evidence that the elliptical building was a residence, and neither did it have any military features. In fact, it was unique to *Deva*, with no equal in any other fortress. Like its neighbour it was also a mystery. One wonders, therefore, if the building had been built by command of the governor as a symbol of Roman greatness to impress the various dignitaries visiting him at the fortress. It was suggested that the twelve rooms may have represented deities or the months of the year, and were used as a place of worship or for conducting ceremonies at certain times of the year. But excavations revealed that partial rebuilding had taken place on the main building and the baths, which were finally built over by modern Chester, and this once regal building now lies beneath the town hall. However, the *Sacellum* of the headquarters building was successfully located and left exposed so that it could be seen through a glass panel outside one of the stores next to the indoor market. This strong room was quite a large one, about six feet long and five feet deep, and like the one at Caernarvon, it had a small flight of steps leading down into it. The surviving grey stonework looks abandoned and trapped in its own time warp.

In another area, the foundations of yet another extensive building came to light. The altars dedicated to Greek doctors identified it as a hospital. References to Greek doctors were not considered unusual since the Romans favoured Greek physicians and recruited them from the Greek-speaking regions of their empire.

At *Deva* the barracks occupied a major part of the fortress, with blocks found at many different places. Only when they had been sited could the rest of the fortress be set out. There were twelve blocks in all, with a separate block for the auxiliary units, which was located on either side of the headquarters building. The legionary quarters were 165 feet long and twenty-eight feet wide and were internally divided into eleven double rooms, each set consisting of a large inner room with bunks for sleeping. Each pair of legionaries also had a smaller outer room for storing equipment. In comparison, the centurions' quarters were eighty-five feet long, with a five-foot alleyway separating each pair. One of the centurion's quarters had a suite of ten rooms with an internal passage, and there was evidence that he had his walls plastered with a floral design. Another block occupied its usual position in the south-west corner of the fortress and was found next to the excavated baths.

An integral part of the fortress was its parade ground. This was located outside its east gate and extended all the way down the eastern defences. In the tenth century, the Queen of Mercia, King Alfred the Great's daughter, was credited with strengthening its decaying walls and extended them down to the river to create a fortified town for the new settlers. Over time, a large civilian population grew up there.

With the fortress being dismantled from around the middle of the third century to the early fourth century, its stonework made suitable building material for the communities

48. The surviving North Wall.

that were also growing up outside the western and southern defences. Already vast quantities of local sandstone had been used for building the fortress, all of which had come from the quarries lying to the south of the river, now known as Handbridge. Although the quarries have been entirely stripped, they have now been transformed into a beautiful parkland known as Edgar's Field.

The most enduring monument to those industrious times is the shrine to Minerva that the soldiers carved into the rock face, which has been preserved for all to see. Minerva was the goddess of wisdom, handicraft and the arts. She was also the goddess of warriors and was adopted by the soldiers to protect them at work; therefore, they made a daily offering at the shrine before quarrying the stone. The shrine, about six feet high, is the only one to have survived in Britain. Over the centuries the figure of Minerva has almost withered away, but parts of the figure are just discernible. Early woodcuts of the shrine show the helmeted Minerva holding a spear in her right hand and with an owl sitting on her left shoulder. Just beyond the shrine is the only surviving block of sandstone in the quarry. It towers above the path running beneath it. Located alongside the river bank, the park is a pleasant place to walk beneath the elder trees. One can imagine what a bustling place it once was. First-century pottery was also found here in large quantities when the large-scale excavations were in progress. The park can be reached by the Old Dee Bridge. The Romans probably had a bridge there too, although they would have found it more convenient to transport the stone by barge and to dock right outside its west gate, where they had built a quay. Since Roman times, the river has changed it course, and it is now located further south, flowing east to west along the southern boundaries of the city.

In 2006, a sandstone quarry was found on land that had been stripped ready for development in the north-east corner of the city. Trenches cut by the visiting archaeologists showed that a solid layer of sandstone lay just three to five feet below the surface. Cut marks in the stone and the finding of Roman pottery confirmed that the Romans had already started to excavate stone from there.

The civilian settlement which had established itself alongside the river outside the western defences flourished into a maritime trading centre with a large harbour, importing goods from the Continent. It had been densely populated and had a number of warehouses as well as

49. Soldiers' Shrine to Minerva.

50. The surviving sandstone rock, now in Edgar's Field.

residential buildings. To the north were workshops and the settlement's cemetery. In the centre of the community were the civic baths. They covered an area of 300 feet square, to make them a third larger than the fortress ones. At excavation, both concrete and herringbone-tile floors were found, as well as mosaic ones. The baths were probably as luxurious as the legionary ones and those at Caerleon. Some of the earliest features of this building suggest it was built not long after the fortress, and that the legion had been involved with its construction. The early provision of baths to a neighbouring civilian population would suggest that the military were anxious to offer those who came into contact with their soldiers to have the same high standards of personal hygiene and cleanliness. As civilians had already begun to settle on the available plots of land around the parade ground, this settlement eventually met those that were established in the south, until they all emerged at the river's edge.

In the southern area, it was found that a series of large, well-built and imposing buildings had existed there from the late first century to the fourth century, most noticeable of which was the amphitheatre, the largest in Roman Britain. It was sited outside the south-east corner of the fortress and must have been an awe inspiring sight to those coming into the city at that point. In fact, the amphitheatre was discovered 'just across the road' from the excavated south-east tower.

## The Amphitheatre

The discovery of this extraordinary building was made by accident when a schoolmaster of the Ursuline Convent School came across its outer wall in the school's cellar while heating was being installed there in 1927. At once, he recognised the stonework to be Roman and informed the authorities. At that time there were plans to straighten the road between New Gate and St John's Church, which meant the work would cut across the amphitheatre's area, but as a result of a public appeal by the Chester Archaeological Society, the plans were amended and sufficient money was raised to commence excavations on the site. This decision was greatly encouraged by the news that work was commencing on the one at Caerleon, and it was considered a matter of civic pride that the one at Chester should also be quickly excavated. But owing to existing buildings occupying the site, only the northern half of the amphitheatre was available for excavation. At first, it was found that St John's House, an old ecclesiastical building associated with the Church of St John, was encroaching

51. The amphitheatre with ongoing excavations.

upon the site, so it was bought by the Chester Archaeological Society for demolition so that excavation could take place.

In 1930 the face of the arena wall was exposed in a number of places, as was the arena itself, which was found to be fourteen feet below ground level and measuring 190 by 162 feet overall. The wall was standing to a height of nine and a half feet, and had originally been covered with primary coats of white lime plaster which had then been painted a dark reddish-brown. At a later date the Roman builders covered the wall with a thicker plaster to hide any cracks or imperfections in the stone.

The arena's natural surface had been covered with a layer of yellow-brown sand, six inches thick, and a few scattered slabs of sandstone set in the sand were thought to have been the original floor. At each end of the long axis were the entrances leading into the arena. The north entrance was investigated in 1960–61, and was seen to be eighteen feet wide at the door end, narrowing to twelve feet where it entered the arena. Around the periphery were subsidiary entrances with flights of steps leading up to the seating terraces and the separate areas reserved for the legion's senior officers and visiting dignitaries. The enclosure was a square-shaped chamber with its walls still intact, and was located at the edge of the eastern side of the arena.

During the 1960s excavations, the most noteworthy discovery was that there were two outer walls; the Romans had built an extra wall eight feet from the inner one to create a much larger amphitheatre. This newer building was therefore capable of seating more spectators, from 5,000 to 7,000. Its walls had also been raised from fifteen to thirty feet. The other difference was that the extended amphitheatre had an external staircase to reach the terraces. The only other amphitheatre with an external staircase is at Pompeii. A quantity of Flavian-dated pottery, and a little worn coin of Vespasian, dated the building of the first amphitheatre to around AD 71. There was reason to believe that the second building may have started as early as AD 80, meaning the Romans took only a few years to change their minds and make it larger.

Recent and ongoing excavations into the seating terraces in the northern half of the amphitheatre produced some interesting finds of animal bones such as chicken legs and beef ribs, which suggested that food vendors were in attendance to supply spectators with a variety of snacks. Another interesting find from 1737 was a gladiatorial scene sketched on a piece of Welsh slate. It showed two combatants fighting, one of whom had a trident in one hand and a net in the other, and it may indicate that gladiatorial fights had taken place there. The sketch also had a perfect representation of a *gladius*, or sword, thus giving valuable information as to the weapons used. Such fights were popular and were often the highlight of a Roman's day out. A miniature Samian bowl decorated with a gladiatorial scene also came to light. It is thought that these tiny bowls may have been sold wholesale as souvenirs to the spectators. A piece that had come off the bone handle of a *gladius*, possibly broken in combat, was also recovered. It was the usual practice after the combats to rake the sand in the arena clean and then dump it outside the amphitheatre walls. Curiously, examination of this sand revealed a human tooth.

A significant discovery by the wall of the first amphitheatre was a painted shrine dedicated to the goddess Nemesis, who was patron goddess of the gladiatorial games. She was also the goddess of vengeance, on whom the Romans called if they wanted a particular favour

– namely a curse or to seek revenge on someone. The *Nemeseum* was discovered close to the main north entrance and consisted of a small stone-built chamber measuring twelve by fourteen feet. Centrally placed at the rear of the room were two bases that had served as plinths for altars or cult figures, but no such figures were present. The missing altar dedicated to Nemesis was found a little distance away and its inscription read:

DEAE NEMESI SEXT MARCIANUS. EX VISV

This translates to:

To the goddess Nemesis, Sextius Marcianus, the Centurion, set this up after a vision.

Another altar was found lying in front of it, and it was possible that the two were moved from their original positions to be included in the newer amphitheatre. The altar to Nemesis measured nineteen by thirteen and a half inches and was ten inches deep. It had been carved out of hard red sandstone with a six-petalled rose design at the top. The altar is now on display at the Grosvenor Museum.

Under the Romans, the amphitheatre continued in use for 200 years, although it fell into disuse for a short period. However, after the Romans left in the late fourth century, it continued to be used for centuries by the incoming civilian population. Late Saxon pottery from around AD 800 was found on the site, and even the remains of timber buildings were found within the arena, thought to have come from the medieval period. Cesspits had also been dug into the area floor during that period – a decorative comb was found in one. A medieval coin also surfaced, as well as a thirteenth-century jug. Two of the amphitheatre's main entrances had been deliberately walled up, which may indicate that the structure was later intended to defend the city. This probably occurred during the Civil War in the seventeenth century. This theory was confirmed by the finding of a lead musket and pistol balls found on the site. Gaming dice from the eighteenth century also emerged.

As time went by, the area surrounding the amphitheatre was much sought after by the wealthy, who built their mansions there. The Church, too, was attracted to the site, and many ecclesiastical buildings were constructed, including St John's Church, which became Chester's first cathedral, and was attended by King Edgar in AD 973. There were also chapels and houses for vicars and canons, all of which, in effect, stopped the overdevelopment of the site and may have preserved at least half of the amphitheatre.

Excavations of the amphitheatre were still in progress during 2006, when daily finds were being sent to the nearby visitors' centre for recording and storage. Conservation of such unique and delicate objects was a painstaking process that required patience and dedication. Most of the bulky materials such as pottery shards were bagged in polythene bags with labels indicating the site code and were often stored in cardboard boxes. Later, attempts were made to match up individual pieces in order to rebuild the object in its original shape. Metal objects were routinely X-rayed and were kept in perforated polythene bags in conditions requiring a consistent temperature and low humidity. No matter where the excavations were, the main concern was always preservation of whatever was found, so at each excavation an expert was always at hand to advise on lifting and handling delicate objects.

52. The shrine to Nemesis found in the amphitheatre.

Just south of the amphitheatre was a temple, and it was thought that a *Mithraeum* might also have been in the vicinity. At such a prestigious site as *Deva*, it is certainly possible that one was built here and was well attended by the expanding population. Close by was a multi-roomed *Mansio*, which had been built in the first century. From what was discovered of its remains, it had a long and chequered history, having been burnt down during the third century and then rebuilt again. Some of the debris and rubble from the fire had been dumped down its two wells, including the body of a young man aged between eighteen and twenty-three who had apparently died in the fire. His skeleton showed that he had broken his leg during his lifetime and had probably walked with a limp, which perhaps had impeded his escape from the flames. The skeleton is also on display at the Grosvenor Museum. A rectangular blue-green glass bottle was also recovered. The *Mansio* was finally demolished during the fourth century.

The incoming settlers even put down their roots two miles south-east of *Deva* at the places we now know as Saltney and Heronbridge.

At Heronbridge, there was evidence of bronze slag, clay crucibles and clay moulds for making bronze objects, clearly indicating that an industrial site had occupied this left bank of the Dee. The buildings included substantial structures partitioned internally into rooms of over thirty to forty feet wide and more than 100 feet long. These strip buildings were thought to have been repositories for goods, and the rooms at their ends used as living quarters. In addition, four buildings about five feet square showed signs that they had produced intense heat, and the presence of grain in one of the stoke holes implied that they had been drying kilns. It is possible that the grain had been destined for the fortress.

The community at Saltney had been much poorer, living in flimsy constructed homes surrounded by fenced and ditched enclosures. Despite the poor quality of the soil, the presence of querns suggested that the people had managed to glean a meagre existence from agriculture by producing grain. The discovery of a high proportion of third- and fourth-century pottery suggested that the community went on to occupy the site until the end of the fourth century. This was the time when some of the troops were removed from Britain during the reign of Magnentius, in AD 350–353.

Around *Deva* itself the individual communities continued to grow in size and importance throughout the coming centuries until the town finally emerged as modern-day Chester.

# About the Author

Sarah Symons was born in the Swansea Valley, South Wales, and grew up in Shrewsbury. She then moved to Aylesbury and started her career as a medical secretary at Stoke Mandeville Hospital. She continued her secretarial career at the BBC and other major companies and attended the House of Lords while private secretary to Lord Greenwood of Rossendale, an ex-cabinet minister. While in London, she became involved with the London Welsh and became Secretary of the London Glamorgan Society for a short while.

Sarah eventually returned to South Wales and now lives in Swansea, where she enjoys writing and travelling. She also loves photography and likes to illustrate her books whenever she can.

She became interested in the Roman era after attending many writing holidays at the University College of Wales at Caerleon, and has enjoyed visiting all the Roman sites throughout Wales.

Her previous publications include *Fortresses and Treasures of Roman Wales* and *The Wonders of Dan yr Ogof* (the National Showcaves Centre for Wales).

# Image Credits

Images 3, 5, 6, 8, 10, 11, 12, 46 reproduced by kind permission of the National Museum & Galleries of Wales; 7, 9 courtesy of the Glamorgan-Gwent Archaeological Trust; 22, 27, 29 courtesy of Newport Museum & Art Gallery; 25, 26, 30 reproduced by kind permission of the Newport Museum & Art Gallery; 31, 34, 35 provided by the Carmarthen County Museum; 36 reproduced by kind permission of Neath and Port Talbot Museum Services; 37, 38 reproduced by kind permission of the National Trust; 41, 42 courtesy of Cadw, Welsh Government; 43 courtesy of jay-jerry, under Creative Commons 2.0 Generic license; 44, 45 courtesy of John McLinden, under Creative Commons 2.0 Generic license; 47, 52 reproduced by kind permission of Grosvenor Museum, Chester.

More Welsh History from Amberley Publishing

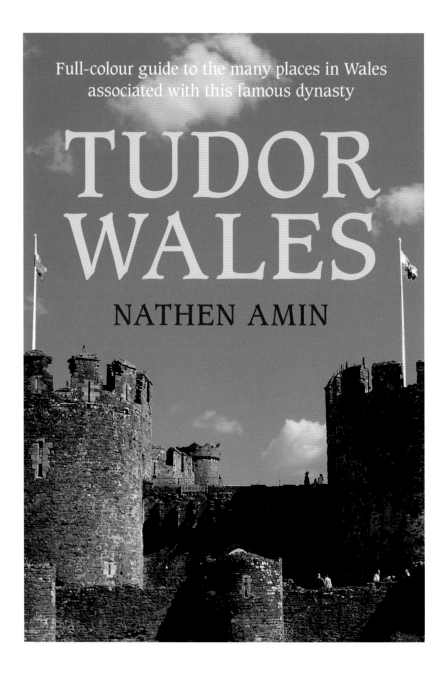

Full-colour guide to the many places in Wales
associated with this famous dynasty

# TUDOR
# WALES

## NATHEN AMIN